THE LAW OF
KINDNESS

THE LAW OF
KINDNESS

SERVING WITH HEART
AND HANDS

with Study Questions

Mary Beeke

"...the law of kindness."
—Proverbs 31:26

"...give to drink unto one of these
little ones a cup of cold water...."
—Matthew 10:42

REFORMATION HERITAGE BOOKS
Grand Rapids, Michigan

Published by
Reformation Heritage Books
2965 Leonard St., NE
Grand Rapids, MI 49525
616-977-0599 / Fax 616-285-3246
e-mail: orders@heritagebooks.org
website: www.heritagebooks.org

First Printing 2007
Second Printing 2008

Library of Congress Cataloging-in-Publication Data

Beeke, Mary.
  The law of kindness : serving with heart and hands / by Mary Beeke.
    p. cm.
  ISBN 978-1-60178-029-4 (pbk. : alk. paper)
  1. Kindness—Religious aspects—Christianity. I. Title.
  BV4647.K5B44 2007
  241'.4—dc22
                                    2007041755

---

*For additional Reformed literature, both new and used, request a free
book list from Reformation Heritage Books at the above address.*

Contents

Dedication

⟫ ••• ⟪

To my precious parents,
Henry and Lena Kamp,
thank you for laying a foundation
of steady service to others and consistent,
genuine kindness in my childhood home.

To my loving husband,
Joel Beeke,
thank you for your constant stream of support
and for your Christ-like kindness to me
and to our children.

To my dear children,
Calvin, Esther, and Lydia,
my heart rejoices to see your kindness,
your patience, and your graciousness.

⟫ ••• ⟪

I thank and praise God for each of you.
I love you. You are more than I deserve.

A Cup of Cold Water

And whosoever shall give to drink unto one of these little ones a cup of cold water only in the name of a disciple, verily I say unto you, he shall in no wise lose his reward.
— Matthew 10:42

Well, I can do as much as that. I can do a kind act toward the Lord's servant. The Lord knows I love them all, and would count it an honor to wash their feet. For the sake of their Master I love the disciples.

How gracious of the Lord to mention so insignificant an action—"to give to drink a cup of cold water only"! This I can do, however poor; this I may do, however lowly; this I will do cheerfully. This, which seems so little, the Lord notices—notices when done to the least of His followers. Evidently it is not the cost, nor the skill, nor the quantity, that He looks at, but the motive: that which we do to a disciple, because he is a disciple, his Lord observes, and recompenses. He does not reward us for the merit of what we do, but according to the riches of His grace.

I give a cup of cold water, and He makes me to drink of living water. I give to one of His little ones, and He treats me as one of them. Jesus finds an apology for His liberality in that which His grace has led me to do, and He says, "He shall in no wise lose his reward."
— Charles H. Spurgeon

Introduction

I can remember it as if it were yesterday, though it was more than thirty-five years ago. It was recess time. A small crowd of junior high students had gathered on the knoll beyond the school. My friends and I were curious. At the center of the group stood one of their classmates, his hands behind his back. They had tied his wrists together so tightly that one hand was sheet white, the other beet red. The bell ended recess. They left him standing in the field.

I was shocked and dismayed, but I was too paralyzed to do anything. I was, after all, four years younger. I left him standing there, too, and I wondered what would happen to him. But I have replayed this scene in my mind countless times. The two things that stand out starkly were the color of his hands and the resigned, almost serene, look on his face. In the replay, though, I am not just standing there. I am kicking and punching the captors and yelling at them with tears and outrage, "Why are you being so mean? Why can't you just be nice?"

This experience and many others, both positive and negative, have instilled in me a deep desire to promote "just plain kindness" in my own life, and beyond, in whatever way I can. There are countless times I have violated this principle, and I apologize to anyone to whom I have been unkind. I have agonized over whether or not I ought even to write a book such as this. Who am I to presume to be an authority on kindness? I am no authority, but I have to write this book. It's burning inside of me. So at the outset I want to make clear that I am writing as a sinner, one who tries to be kind but still falls short. I love kindness, but I am still striving to live up to all I have written. And I'm sure I will be doing that for the rest of my life. That being said, it is my fervent prayer and desire that God will bless this book to foster more kindness among our fellow human beings in this world.

I have been surrounded by very kind people my entire life. This is a tremendous blessing. It is also a responsibility. When I was a child, my mother, usually with a cheerful smile on her face, cared for us, brought meals to sick friends, chatted with anybody anywhere, volunteered for various causes, and showed hospitality in our home. She is still doing these things and more today. Now she is also "the blanket lady," buying blankets by the dozen at garage sales and estate sales, washing them, and distributing them around the world through whatever organization can use them.

I remember my father, in his quiet and solemn way, serving in church and school, donating blood, never allowing us to speak ill of anyone, treating every person with respect (even if they were "different"), and donating money to a variety of worthy causes. He has always seen the positive side of others, and he expects the best of them, even when they have a track record that shows evidence to the contrary. He's still serving today, and by now he has donated fourteen gallons of blood.

Then there is my husband. He's the best husband in the world. Joe overflows with kindness and love. Joe has never said one unkind word to me. He exudes kindness to me and to our children. When I'm irritable or frustrated, he is the stabilizing factor in our home. In his ministry as a pastor, his kindness is a consistent thread woven through his words and actions. I have never met anyone who has endured the variety of afflictions that he has in his life and remained kind throughout. This kindness and love pervades his thought patterns and affects both his public and private life. Because of his pastoral and personal experiences, I've asked him to write the part of this book relating to kindness in marriage from the perspective of a husband.

I am not the same person today as when I set out to write this book. I have needed to dissect my beliefs in order to explain them on paper. In doing so, some of my attitudes have changed. My attitudes must be guided by the same principles professed in this book. Necessity dictated that I return to the Bible each time because God designed and created us, and it is through His eyes and mind that we must interpret the world that He has created.

This is a Christian book. But it is also a book for and about non-Christians. (I use this term "non-Christian" for lack of a better—no ill intended.) It is impossible to get at the heart of kindness any other way than through God, for He is the essence of true kindness. There is only one God. He is the God of heaven and earth. He is the God of justice; He punishes sin. But He is also the God of mercy and kindness; He forgives and cleanses all who come to Him truly repenting of their sin and believing on Jesus. The kindness of Jesus is reflected in His followers because He writes the "law of kindness" on their hearts (Prov. 31:26).

Showing kindness and love to others is at the very center of the life of a Christian.

The exclusivity of Christianity may be very offensive to some of you. I cannot have a dialogue with each of you; I only ask, if you do not espouse Christianity, that you at least read the Bible. As you read, try to ascertain the reasons you don't believe. Try to determine the personality of Jesus Christ. May I suggest that you begin with John 8:1-11 and Luke 10: 25-37? Any person who really knows Jesus cannot help but love Him.

Try God out. With an open mind and an open heart pray, "God, if Thou art real, please show me." With all the love of my heart, I hope and pray you will experience the loving power of God in your life. Jesus was the most compassionate man who ever walked the face of the earth; you will see that from the way He treated those who were down and out. He is the only possible source of true joy and peace for your life. If you ever get in a really tight spot in your life, remember God; He is the best source of help available.

Believing in God is not optional. It's a matter of *when* we believe (see Rom. 14:11-12). If we don't believe now, we will believe on the Day of Judgment. But then we will experience the reality of God in His anger, and it will be too late to experience His kindness and mercy. It is kind of Jesus to warn you now, before it is too late. If you were traveling on an expressway and came to a roadblock, you might be irritated. But if you were told the bridge ahead had just collapsed, your irritation would turn to heart-felt gratitude. It is precisely this emotion that many new Christians feel when they realize they have been snatched from the jaws of hell by the kindness and mercy of Jesus

Christ. Roger Roberts states, "Though kindness does not preclude judgment yet kindness is always presented as God's preference over judgment. His desire is that none perish, but all come to repentance, and Isaiah 28:21 notes that judgment is His 'strange work,' that which is a work of necessity (necessitated by His perfect justice), whereas kindness is His delightful attitude and forgiveness and grace His delightful work"[1] (see Micah 7:18).

I care about each one of you. I would like every person to be kind. This world would be a better place. But kindness alone will not save your soul. Only Jesus Christ can do that. It is my sincere hope and prayer that God will bring this great kindness to you. Meanwhile, let's be kind—all of us, no matter who, no matter what.

This book is divided into three parts. The first is called "Kindness Examined," and in its three chapters we will define kindness, explain where kindness comes from, and then examine specific motives for kindness. The second section, "Kindness Learned," deals with the development of kindness in the areas of marriage and parenting. The section continues with the teacher's role in promoting kindness. Bullying is specifically addressed. Chapter nine is a letter to children and teens on the subject of kindness and unkindness. "Kindness in Action," the third part, addresses kind and unkind thoughts and words. Next, kindness to those who are less privileged is covered. The concluding chapter is entitled, "Your kind of kindness."

Kindness can be described better with examples than with definitions; therefore, I have tried to provide stories throughout this book to express what kindness is. I have changed the names of some of the individuals in the stories.

All the negative examples, stories of unkindness, have the identities changed out of kindness to spare the guilty and the mistaken. Some of the names are changed in the positive stories. All changed names appear in quotation marks. Some state only the first name with or without an initial, and some are identified fully. Names from news stories remain the same. Some examples are hypothetical situations that happen in everyday life.

I would like to thank several individuals who have contributed in various ways to this book. My heartfelt gratitude goes to Martha Fisher for her invaluable editing, to Kate DeVries for her proofreading, to Gary and Linda den Hollander for their typesetting, and to Amy Zevenbergen for producing the cover. My apologies to all those who have asked me to lend a hand and to whom I have had to answer, "I'm sorry, I'm too busy. I have a project I'm working on at home." I hope to be available soon—I can't wait to get out there and practice what I'm preaching! I have mentioned the example and instruction of my parents. My heart is full of gratitude for all they have done. I hope I can repay them by raising their grandchildren by the same principles. Thanks to the sea of kind people in our own church and those we have met everywhere we go, especially those who have prayed for my husband's ministry and our family. They have warmed our hearts and given inspiration to pass their kindness on.

A truckload of gratitude is due to my precious children, Calvin, Esther, and Lydia. I thank them for the ideas they have contributed to this book by way of dinnertime discussions, and thanks to Esther for suggesting the title. Our children have unwittingly spurred me on in the area of kindness. Our own families know us best. So I thank them for their forbearance, love, support, and kindness in spite of all my shortcomings and inconsistencies. They have been truly kind to me. I thank the Lord for this and for the kindness I see them pass on to others. It touches my heart to the core.

Words fail to express my gratitude to my dear husband, Joe, for his steadfast love and tenacious support of me. He has encouraged me to continue writing about this subject that I love so much, in spite of times when I felt completely unworthy to do so. He has overlooked dust and clutter and has offered to take the family out to eat more times than he probably should have, so I could have time to write. I am deeply grateful to God for this man who lives by the law of kindness.

---

1. Roger Roberts, *Holiness: Every Christian's Calling* (Nashville: Broadman Press, 1985), 68.

PART 1
Kindness Examined

CHAPTER 1
What is Kindness?

Kindness happens.

Heidi was attempting to exit the mall. Her two toddlers were tired, hungry, crying, and trying to escape from the stroller. The automatic door opener didn't work, and the wind whipped the door shut. A middle-aged mom, with no children in tow, held the door as Heidi and her children passed through.

Coby van Rossum worked in Nigeria as a nurse, midwife, and health instructor from 1964 to 1987. At the age of 60, she was required by her mission board to retire. But she had no desire to stop working. Instead, she focused her energy on helping the disabled individuals with whom she had been working, and Project Elim was born. Today, Elim serves over a thousand individuals in a community-based rehabilitation program. Field workers visit the villages to find physically and mentally handicapped persons. They decide on a treatment plan, which may include surgery, physical therapy, or occupational therapy. They may equip the individual with a wheelchair, special shoes, or another appliance. Family members accompany the disabled person during his or her time away from home. Finally, he or she is trained for an occupation that can be performed at home, in the community, or at Elim itself. Elim has a staff of fifty and raises funds through a restaurant, a shop, a bakery, and a guesthouse. In 1999, Elim added an AIDS program. Many previously rejected disabled people are now contributing citizens of their community.[1]

Unkindness happens.

On August 28, 2001, a 28-year-old woman stood on the edge of a 160-foot-high bridge in Seattle, Washington. As people drove by in cars, trucks, and buses, some yelled at her to jump. She did. After bobbing to the surface, she was taken to a hospital in serious condition.[2]

On April 26, 2002, in Erfurt, Germany, Robert Steinhauser opened fire in the school from which he had been expelled, killing thirteen teachers, a secretary, two students, and a policeman.[3]

Kindness happens in the face of unkindness.

On September 11, 2001, four passenger airplanes were turned into weapons of mass destruction as American Airlines Flight 11 and United Airlines Flight 175 were flown into the World Trade Center towers, American Airlines Flight 77 was flown into the Pentagon, and United Airlines Flight 93 crashed in Pennsylvania. The death toll was 3021.[4] As Americans reacted with grief, shock, and horror, they also moved to action. Volunteers from near and far converged on New York City, helping in any way possible. They rescued the living and they carried out the dead. They gave water to rescue workers and rescue dogs. They prayed to God and comforted mourning strangers. They donated blood. They donated millions of dollars to disaster relief organizations. People from around the world sent their condolences.

Kindness happens every day in small ways and in large

ways all over the world. So does unkindness. Only God sees all, and only He knows the balance between the two.

What is kindness? How is it manifested? Why be kind? Why do some people exude kindness and others lack even a shadow of it? What motivates kindness? Can it be learned or is it an intrinsic character trait? How much is learned from example and instruction? Is there an ideal age to learn to be kind? How much should we be concerned with it? Is it an essential or an extra? Why can't everybody just be nice?

These questions and more need to be answered. Their answers are manifold. Let's begin by defining kindness, and then continue by looking at how it is manifested, the varying degrees of kindness, and its importance.

Definition

What is kindness? Webster's Dictionary defines it as "the state, quality, or habit of being kind; kind act or treatment; kind feeling; affection; good will."[5] Synonyms of kindness are compassion, gentleness, benevolence, thoughtfulness, mercy, consideration, and helpfulness. Unkindness is defined as "not being sympathetic to or considerate of others; harsh, severe, cruel, rigorous, etc."[6] Dissecting these definitions, we see that kindness consists of two parts: first, the feelings of compassion and motives of our hearts, and second, the resulting behavior that is intended for the improvement of another person's situation. Thus, kindness includes what is on the inside and is invisible to others, and what is exhibited and is visible to others. Scripture refers to the first as kindness and the second as goodness. Jerry Bridges explains that "kindness is the sincere desire for the happiness of others; goodness is the activity calculated to advance that happiness."[7] For our purposes, I will use *kindness* and *acts of kindness* interchangeably, with the context making the meaning clear.

William J. Bennett describes compassion as "a virtue that takes seriously the reality of other persons, their inner lives, their emotions, as well as their external circumstances. It is an active disposition toward fellowship and sharing, toward supportive companionship in distress or in woe."[8] Kindness flows from the heart and is focused on the needs of another. Betty Huizenga says that kindness is "showing personal care and concern in meeting the needs of others." She emphasizes that this is an attitude and a conscious decision that requires a person to put forth effort to act upon this attitude.[9]

Manifestation of kindness

Kindness manifests itself in words, actions, and nonverbal behavior. A cheerful mother serving supper to her family and asking them about their day is a picture of kindness. She asks, "How did your math test go? Did you play with Joshua? Did your sales rep stop by today?" Her actions are kind: squeezing a shoulder, serving Marie's favorite meal because it's her birthday, and noticing when Steve needs a napkin. Her nonverbal gestures are kind: smiling, attentively listening to whoever is speaking, and using a pleasant tone of voice.

Attending a youth camp is something that teens usually would rather not do alone. They like the emotional support of a companion. Karen felt that way, too, but she had no companion. She decided to brave it alone. On the bus ride down, she was a quiet island in a sea of noise. She took her bags to her cabin and headed to the opening activities. On the way she met Mandy, who was also walking alone. Mandy introduced herself and asked Karen to join her for the games. Just a few words in a particular situation put Karen at ease and dissolved her worries. Proverbs 25:11 reminds us that "a word fitly spoken is like apples of gold in pictures of silver."

Kind actions can also be wordless. Chris told me of a Saturday morning breakfast of waffles with a friend who had stayed overnight. Instead of using a knife and fork, the visitor simply picked up the waffle and ate it with his hands, syrup dripping from all sides. Chris' mom is very proper and very clean, but more than that, she is kind. When she observed the visitor, she proceeded to eat her waffle in the same manner. Her teenage sons were flabbergasted, but their visitor felt very much at home.

A story of silent kindness appears in the Bible. Shem and Japheth walked backwards as they covered the nakedness of their father, Noah, in contrast to Ham, who didn't look away and didn't cover his father, but instead told his brothers what he had seen. To protect someone's dignity during a moment of shame is kindness.

There is an infinite number of ways to demonstrate kindness to our fellow human beings. We have many opportunities every day. If we have the law of kindness in our hearts and other sinful factors or emotions are not overshadowing this principle, then our behavior will be flavored with kindness.

Varying degrees

Kindness is a broad concept. People exhibit kindness in

varying degrees, from small, almost imperceptible acts to life-encompassing acts. A truly kind person shows kindness habitually, in addition to performing purposeful acts of kindness. He or she shows care and concern for others and their needs and interests. A kind person does not play favorites but instead respects every individual as a created being. He or she is not sarcastic and will not take joy in the calamity of another.

However, the kind person is not wishy-washy. He is honest even when it causes pain, and he stands firmly on biblical principles even when it is unpopular. The Christian loves the Lord above all, and God's law reflects God Himself. Therefore, kindness subjects itself to God's law, maintaining standards of right and wrong. In essence, morality and kindness go hand in hand. The deepest motive of kindness stems from humility and gratitude to God for His wonderful gift of salvation. This person says, "God showed me unparalleled kindness by forgiving my sins; I will be kind to others in return, whether they are kind or unkind to me."

Even among those whom we would label as truly kind, there is incredible diversity. A little grandma in a prairie town who saw fifteen people in an average week and Corrie ten Boom were both kind, but the scope of each life was vastly different. A truly kind person might be very busy with life's duties but infuses kindness along the way wherever he or she goes, perhaps by allowing a fellow driver into his or her lane or by smiling at an awkward teen fumbling for her money in the checkout lane. There are millions of individuals who dedicate a few hours every week to a favorite charity, from leading a boy scout troop, to counseling at a crisis pregnancy center, to teaching Sunday school, to serving meals in a homeless shelter. There are untold numbers of individuals, many of them retirees, who spend most of their waking hours volunteering in hospitals, building homes for Habitat for Humanity, or sitting by the beds of the dying in a hospice home. There are also those who make it their life's work to care for others and show kindness, whether it be the "angel of mercy" nurse in the local hospital, the helpful janitor at school, or the Red Cross worker in war-torn Afghanistan.

There is a distinction between kindness as a character trait and isolated acts of kindness, though the line between the two is nebulous. The first is pervasive, with a direct link between kind motives and kind actions. The latter is more sporadic, and kind deeds may or may not be linked to kind motives. Even unkind people show kindness once in a while. "Madeline" has issues with each neighbor and is rude to all of them, but when her gardening friends stop by, she is full of warm congeniality.

Within each of us lies a kaleidoscope of experiences, memories, personal relationship skills, motives, character traits, moods, principles, and feelings. These can converge into a great variety of behaviors. Identical behaviors can stem from different motives in different individuals. Jake might be raking leaves with the church youth group because he empathizes with elderly folks who are unable to do their yard work, while Blake might be raking leaves because his parents are compelling him to do so. The outcome is the same though the thought process is not.

Even in the same individual, the motive may be different from time to time. When I told "Nancy" how I admired her for consistently helping a widow friend, she said, "Sometimes I do it because I care for her and love her because Christ loved me, but other times it's just duty that drives me."

It is possible that each ingredient, kind motives and kind actions, could occur independently. A person could have kindness in his or her heart, but no one would benefit from it unless it was acted upon. A totally introverted or isolated person could possibly be kind and not show it. It seems, though, that if kindness is in the heart, it will reveal itself even if the individual is not purposefully kind. "Hilda" is a bit like that. She is extremely shy, works very well in the family business, and never speaks unless spoken to. At times she seems to be preoccupied in her own little world. Yet when someone speaks to her with warmth, the sweetest smile comes out, and when she gives a gift it is one that is made with her hands and with love.

On the other hand, one could perform an act of kindness for a totally selfish reason. Of all the mission trips that have ever taken place, I wonder how many young people have gone solely because they were interested in a member of the opposite sex who had also signed up to go. Though the motive isn't pure, the behavior is still beneficial. I must admit I've done similar things myself. In fact, maybe we do more of this than we care to admit. Anyway, the Lord can use these experiences of ours in mysterious ways, like causing us to find Him along the way or allowing us to discover the joy of serving others.

There is the possibility that kindness lives in the inner recesses of a person's heart but other character traits overshadow it. "James" is a very nice boy at home and in the neighborhood, but at school he craves attention so strongly that he will be cruel to the younger children in order to be accepted by his peers.

The behavior of humanity is like the sea, constantly moving, mixing, and coming into contact with new people under different conditions. Our lives are fluid as well. The degree to which we are kind is determined by our experiences, our personality, and how we have been instructed by God and others.

How important is kindness?

How much kindness do we need? Is it an essential or an extra in life? A variety of people would give a variety of answers to these questions. Yet most would agree on this: we want *others* to be kind to *us*. Jesus perceived this common thread in human thinking when He instructed, "And as ye would that men should do to you, do ye also to them likewise" (Luke 6:31). To follow the Golden Rule requires each of us to understand our own desires for kind treatment from others, as well as to be cognizant of our neighbor's desire for the same. Then we must place as much value on our neighbor's desire as we do on our own. But thoughts and understanding aren't enough; action is required. Kindness results when we care about others, when we have empathy for them, when our desire is that their needs be met, when their pain becomes our pain and their burden ours, when we put our feelings into action by shouldering part of their load, and when their happiness is promoted by our behavior.

The Golden Rule is founded on the Ten Commandments. But which commandment teaches us to be kind?

All of them do. Jesus instructed us: "Love the Lord thy God with all thy heart, and with all thy soul, and with all thy mind. This is the first and great commandment. And the second is like unto it. Thou shalt love thy neighbor as thyself. On these two commandments hang all the law and the prophets" (Matt. 22:40). W. Phillip Keller points out that "throughout the Scriptures the great theme of God's unrelenting kindness throbs like a powerful heartbeat. 'His merciful kindness is great toward us...' (Ps. 117:2), is a refrain that never dies. It is repeated scores of times as a reminder that the mercy, compassion, and kindness of God flow to us freely, abundantly in refreshing rivers every day."[10] When God's mercy and kindness flow into us, we cannot help but pass it on to others. Consequently, God identifies kindness as a very important characteristic of a Christian. Colossians 3:12 reads, "Put on therefore, as the elect of God, holy and beloved, bowels of mercies, kindness, humbleness of mind, meekness, longsuffering."

The life of Jesus, whose example we are to follow, was a panorama of kindness. He healed the sick, forgave sinners, raised the dead, comforted the needy, and fed the hungry. And to whom did He direct His kindness? Not to the wealthy, the proud, and the socially esteemed, but to the poor, the sick, the rejected ones, the children, the insane, the prostitutes, the deformed, the injured, the dying, the sinners. And He told us that, when we help the needy, it is as if we are showing kindness to Christ Himself.

Jesus did not tolerate those who took advantage of the underprivileged. He became very angry with the money-changers who swindled from those going to the temple. They were defiling God's house. He threw them out to bring back God's honor to His house. He also disdained those who were proud of their own righteousness; the reason again was man's usurping of God's glory. His was righteous anger, and it was for the good of all.

Kindness is foundational in our lives. Its law must be written on our hearts. It is a characteristic that cannot be compartmentalized. "Today I will practice kindness from 4:00 to 5:00 p.m." does not work. Rather, it should color most of what we do. Like drops of food coloring in a glass of water, our actions must be tinted with kindness.

Is kindness important? We would all agree that it is. We can be more effective in what we do when we assimilate the principle of kindness. Family life flows more smoothly with kindness. School goes easier with kindness. The many hours spent at work are calmer when infused with kindness. And social relationships flourish when colored with kindness. This is a practical purpose for being kind, and it will serve us well. But on a more profound level, when we are kind because of God's working His kindness through us, we serve God and bring honor to Him.

1. Cobie van Rossum, *News from Nigeria*, July 2002.
2. "Woman rescued after drivers prod her to jump from bridge," *Grand Rapids Press*, August 29, 2001, A6.
3. Jochen Wiesigal, "18 Killed in massacre at German school," *Grand Rapids Press*, April 26, 2002, A1–A2.
4. Sara Kugler, "Trade center death toll drops," *Grand Rapids Press*, October 12, 2002, A7.
5. David B. Guralnik, ed., *New World Dictionary of the American Language*, Second Edition (Cleveland, Ohio: William Collins Publishers, Inc., 1980), 776.
6. Ibid., 1553.
7. Jerry Bridges, *The Practice of Godliness* (Colorado Springs: Navpress, 1983), 231.

8. William J. Bennett, ed., *The Book of Virtues* (New York: Simon & Schuster, 1993), 107.

9. Betty Huizenga, *Apples of Gold* (Colorado Springs: Cook Communications Ministries, 2000), 32–33.

10. W. Phillip Keller, *A Gardener Looks at the Fruits of the Spirit* (Milton Keynes, England: Word Publishing, 1986), 127–28.

CHAPTER 2

The Roots of Kindness

The roots of a tree lie unseen in the earth, where they do their work of storing food and drawing water and nourishment from the soil to help the fruit grow. Likewise, the roots of kindness lie deep within the mind and the soul of a person, giving rise to the fruit of kindness. What are these movements in the soul that produce kindness? Where do they originate? What is the difference between the purer forms of kindness and those that are less pure?

The fruit of the Spirit is love, joy, peace, long-suffering, gentleness, goodness, faith, meekness, and temperance (Gal. 5:22–23). Kindness is intimately interwoven into all of these. It is a good work. According to Scripture, a good work is defined not only by the visible behavior (the fruit), but also by the motive of the heart (the root). The Heidelberg Catechism draws from several parts of Scripture and describes good works as "only those [works] which proceed from a true faith, are performed according to the law of God, and to His glory; and not such as are founded on our imaginations or the institutions of men."[1] There are two types of roots that produce good works in general and kindness in particular. The first is the root of saving grace, which produces true saving faith and truly kind acts.

The second is the root of common grace, which produces outwardly good works but lacks true saving faith.

The root of saving grace

God's gift of saving grace in the life of a Christian produces true saving faith. This causes him to repent of his sin and trust completely in the Lord Jesus Christ for salvation. The Holy Spirit fills his heart with the fruit of the Spirit, and love is at the center of his redirected life. This love, with kindness, shines like a light, back to God and to his neighbor. Thus God is the author of kindness, and He shares it with His people. He *is* kindness. Jesus Christ was kindness personified when He walked this earth for thirty-three years, and Christians have been following in His footsteps, albeit imperfectly, ever since. When the Spirit of God plants this wonderful grace in the heart of a Christian, beautiful kindness springs up. In its purest form, a thoroughly kind deed flows from a heart made kind by the Holy Spirit.

Pure kindness

David and Jonathan were best friends. They promised they would always take care of each other and each other's families. After Jonathan died and David had been king for some time, David wanted to know whether or not any of Jonathan's family were still living. He was told that a son, Mephibosheth, lived in Lodebar; he was lame in both his feet from having been dropped as a child while escaping during a war. King David summoned him. Mephibosheth was very afraid because the kings of that day normally eliminated the entire family of the previous king in order to remove any threat to their thrones. As he bowed before King David, he heard the amazing words, "Fear not: for I will surely show thee kindness for Jonathan thy father's sake, and will restore thee all the land of Saul thy [grand]father; and thou shalt eat bread at my table continually" (2 Sam. 9:7). This was an act of pure kindness.

What are the ingredients of pure kindness? Let's return to the Heidelberg Catechism definition and look at its three parts.

True faith

The first is true faith. "Whatsoever is not of faith is sin," reads Romans 14:23. The converse is that the only sinless behavior is that which is done from true saving faith. Since only a Christian can possess true faith, only a Christian can exercise good works and pure kindness.

This may seem harsh, but if we go back to God's attributes, it makes perfect sense. God is perfectly holy, and He requires us to be perfectly holy also. We have all sinned and we even enjoy it. Because He made us, He has the right to say, "Ye shall be holy, for I am holy" (Lev. 11:44). Sadly, it's too late for us to be holy; we already have a bad record and we still have a bad heart.

But there is hope! Not only is God perfectly holy, He is merciful and gracious as well. He is so kind as to give us His Word and ministers to explain it, so that we can learn that there is a way to escape the punishment of hell for our sins. God the Father sent His Son, Jesus Christ, to live without sin on this earth and then to die a painful, humiliating death on the cross in order to take the punishment for sin. He sincerely offers Himself to those who ask (Luke 11:13; Matt. 7:7). For these reasons, God can call us to pure good works and hold us responsible when we don't heed the call.

According to God's law and not our own imagination

God puts a high premium on obedience. Forging our own path is disobedience and is an insult to Him. In the Old Testament, Israelites could be put to death for disobeying the Ten Commandments. These laws still require our obedience today, but we don't have to die for them. Jesus has come, and He died for our disobedience if we are believers. He also brought a new law, the law of love. We are to love God above all and our neighbor as ourselves (Matt. 22:37–40). The believer overflows with gratitude to God for His gift of salvation, and this results in loving the law and following it from the heart. So good works and acts of pure kindness need to fall within the parameters of the Ten Commandments and the law of love.

To God's glory

"Whatsoever ye do, do all to the glory of God" (1 Cor. 13:31). *Whatsoever* means everything—no exceptions. God deserves glory because He created all things and He rules over all. The believer earnestly wants to place God on the throne. The act of glorifying God necessarily implies that those who glorify Him are in a humble position. Humility induces a Christian to show gratitude to God for His gift of saving grace, and the overflow results in humility and kindness to his neighbor as well. Humility makes the believer realize he still sins, though he resists it. He is not superior to other human beings, just forgiven and blessed. Humility causes the believer to forgive others, to hold no grudges, and to be kind to enemies.

In sum, good works fit a precise definition, but they are not a burden to believers performed out of stiff, intellectual obligation. Not at all! If we are Christians, it is love that gives flavor to our lives. We echo David's song in Psalm 119:97: "O how love I Thy law!" We love righteousness and purity. We love God and His precious gifts to us, especially the gift of our salvation. We love to glorify God in any possible way. We love to serve God. We are courageous to stand up for what is right. We love our neighbor, especially those who are less privileged. We love and care for each soul with whom we come into contact. This is not a life of restriction and boredom; it's a life brimful with freedom and joy!

Saved sinner but still impure

David was called a man after God's own heart. He had numerous godly characteristics, but he was not perfect. In fact, he committed a major act of unkindness that marred the rest of his life.

One evening, when his army was at war and he was strolling on his rooftop, he spied a beautiful woman while she was bathing. He had his servants bring Bathsheba to him, even though he had other wives and she was married to Uriah. That moment of giving in to his lust resulted in a child being conceived. When David found out, he naturally tried to cover it up. He arranged for Uriah to come home from battle to spend some time with his wife so the child would appear to be Uriah's. That scheme failed when Uriah, a man of honor and integrity, refused to spend the night enjoying his wife while his comrades were in battle. David's backup plan was to have Uriah strategically placed at the front of the battle. This plan worked: Uriah was killed, and David took Bathsheba to be his wife (2 Sam. 11).

But God was very displeased and sent Nathan the

prophet to tell David a story (2 Sam. 12:1–14). It was about
a poor shepherd who had one sheep that he loved so much
that he treated it like his own child. A rich man, the owner
of a great flock of sheep, took the poor man's only sheep
for his meal. David was indignant at the rich man and said
that he must be killed. But Nathan pointed out that David
himself was that man. David suddenly recognized his sin for
what it was. God made him suffer many consequences for
the rest of his life. The child died. Violence did not cease to
plague his family. His own son tried to seize his kingship.
His neighbors took his wives. And God's name and cause
were compromised.

David was a saved person, and God never allows His
people to slip out of His hands. But David sinned: he lied
and he committed adultery and murder. As believers, we
fall, too, in a variety of ways and degrees. By doing so, we
tarnish the cause of Christ and bring shame to ourselves.
How do we understand David's situation? These works
were not done in faith but in unbelief. They were not done
according to the Ten Commandments or the law of love,
but according to sinful human desires. They were not to the
glory of God, but for David's glory. Therefore, they certainly
were not good works.

Happily, that was not the end of the story for David or
for us. God accepted David's repentance, and He delayed
and softened some of the punishment. He always accepts
our sincere repentance, even though He may allow the
natural consequences of our sin to take their toll. He is
a gracious, forgiving God who allows us to keep coming
back. He is kind and merciful. While the scars remain,
His forgiving Spirit softens our hearts and motivates us to

repent and to learn from our sins, put them behind us, and move on to genuine good works.

The root of common grace

A rich, young ruler came to Jesus and asked Him what he must do to inherit eternal life. Jesus replied, "Do not commit adultery, Do not kill, Do not steal, Do not bear false witness, Defraud not, Honour thy father and mother" (Mark 10:19). The young man stated that he had done all these things from when he was young. Jesus was moved with love because the man earnestly loved what was good, but Jesus also knew his heart. There was one problem: "One thing thou lackest: go thy way, sell whatsoever thou hast, and give to the poor, and thou shalt have treasure in heaven: and come, take up the cross, and follow me" (Mark 10:21). But the man wasn't willing to give up his wealth; with sadness, he walked away from Jesus.

The rich, young ruler has many peers today. We meet them everywhere. We read about them in the newspapers. They do many good works. They are kind. Their lives are filled with serving others. They are generous. They are friendly and sensitive to the needs of others. But they don't believe in the Lord Jesus Christ. If everything done outside of faith is sin, how do we explain this apparent contradiction? It is God's gift of common grace to mankind.

All people were created in the image of God. Even after Adam and Eve sinned in the Garden of Eden, God allowed many vestiges of goodness to continue. We have beauty in nature. Many countries are governed fairly. Seasons return each year (Gen. 8:22). Nature is consistent. Life continues. People realize there is a God that created

everything they see. Most people understand the Golden
Rule and follow it at least some of the time. Everybody is
born with a conscience, and many people listen to it (Rom.
2:14–15). Most people live peaceably with their neighbors
(Luke 6:32–34).

All this goodness happens because of God's common
grace. God would rather extend His mercy and patience
than His anger and justice (Micah 7:18; Isa. 48:9). He
patiently bears with sinners and their ignorance (Acts
17:30a). He gives an opportunity for people everywhere to
repent (Luke 13:34; Acts 17:30b). God gives good things to
all people (Ps. 145:8–9).

God has a purpose in extending His common grace
to sinners. In 2 Peter 3:9, we read, "The Lord is not slack
concerning his promise, as some men count slackness; but
is longsuffering to us-ward, not willing that any should
perish, but that all should come to repentance." He aims to
draw them to Himself, and His goodness is just one means
He uses to do this. If we are Christians, we ought to pray
that kind unbelievers might realize their good works are
not meritorious and that they might experience the deeper
joy that is to be found in a life of following Christ.

Even though God esteems the faithful, good works of
believers as higher than the good works of non-believers,
it doesn't mean Christians can gloat. Our faith and works
are gifts of God, and they leave no room for boasting. The
kindness of non-Christians ought to humble us if we are
Christians, because sometimes it shines more brightly than
ours does. God alone is the judge of the heart and we must
walk with kindness to all, learn from others' kindness, and
esteem the kindness of others as a gift of God's grace.

Absence of common grace

Unkindness, hate, anger, violence, murder, chaos, and anarchy: when people lack even a remnant of common grace, the results are devastating. It's in the news every day, and it is tragic. People are hurt. Families are ruined. Society unravels. Wars rage. Why does this happen? It's because of depravity, sin, and Satan.

God does run out of patience. He does let people go eventually. Often it happens gradually. By repeatedly ignoring the callings of the conscience, we can become numb to the evil of sin and fall deeper into it. By being surrounded by wicked influences—for example, violent entertainment, political or cultural incitement to evil, or living in an environment of abuse—we can be drawn further away from God and closer to Satan. Satan is an enemy of God and His grace, and he will do anything in his power to promote evil. The seeds of evil find fertile ground in our sinful hearts. Without God's restraining power, we would all go down that road. But thanks be to God, His grace is still available. Let's all make haste to Him for our life's sake.

Pure kindness flows from God's saving grace and colors our lives with a joy that can be winsomely contagious. Others can be attracted to our God through us. His law is upheld and His Name is honored. Is this the kind of kindness you and I are expressing? Are we glorifying God? With heavenly blessing, the cycle of God's grace manifested in believers drawing sinners to Christ can be repeated over and over.

---

1. Heidelberg Catechism, Q. 91.

CHAPTER 3

Our Motives

From the roots grow the fruits. As there are many varieties of fruit, so there are many varieties of kindness. We have all done acts of kindness with ulterior motives to promote ourselves, and we have all expressed genuine kindness for the benefit of our neighbor. As we examine our motives, we'll check our kindness pulse to see if our motives are pure and to adjust our attitude when necessary. This chapter describes acts of kindness stemming from various motives ranging from those prompted by a mixture of selflessness and selfishness to those that are more altruistic.

Kindness for personal gain

Wayne sells robotics to the auto industry. It is a very competitive field, so he pours much energy into gaining customers. He sends them birthday cards and is gregarious over fine dinners and on the phone. He takes some golfing and even attended the soccer game of a client's son. Meanwhile, Wayne's wife pleads with him for more attention and time. He usually misses his own daughter's volleyball games, and he is grouchy at home.

"Antonio" has an up-and-down relationship with his parents. He often speaks to them with disdain. When they require him to work around the house, he reacts with defiance and doesn't do the work. But when he needs to borrow cash or his car needs repairs, he speaks very sweetly to his parents and willingly does whatever they ask him to do. He appreciates their help and he tells his parents he loves them, but he soon returns to his cantankerous behavior.

Kindness for personal gain does not have the well-being of others as its end goal. It has its eye on the benefits to be gained for self. There is an element of the adage "you scratch my back, I'll scratch yours" in the business world, but if the kindness lasts only as long as the "benefits" last, or if someone causes his family to suffer for his personal advancement, it is not thoroughgoing kindness. True kindness remains honest, open, and kind to all.

In the home setting, we are often less kind to our closest kin. If this is our weakness, we must exercise self-control by being as civil and fair at home as we are to our friends. To be kind at home only for our selfish gains is nothing short of using our family, which is meanness, not kindness. Prayer, self-discipline, instruction from the Bible, and the power of the Holy Spirit are required to bulldoze this character trait into extinction.

Preferential kindness

The "Jones" family is a tight-knit clan. They are extremely loving and generous to family members and close friends. They are civil to people they meet in public. But they are unfriendly to their acquaintances with whom they have had disagreements in the past. Instead of allowing past grievances to die peacefully, they continually stir them up by making them the center of family discussions. Their children catch the fire of their convictions and keep the enmity alive.

"Mrs. Miller" is in the middle of venting her frustrations on her child when the phone rings. In a moment, her voice changes from being laced with anger to being laced with honey. She carries out a sweet conversation with her friend, but she returns to her sullen disposition after she hangs up the phone.

Preferential kindness plays the game of favoritism. It may be genuine and generous, but it's not universal. There may be individual acts of kindness, but that is not thoroughgoing, impartial kindness. With clan-directed kindness, the positive result is often family closeness and loyalty. But the negative result is arrogance and spite passed down through the generations. While stepping on others—whether it is those of another race, religion, or class—they elevate themselves. There are Christian families who do this, but it is not a Christian virtue. In fact, the opposite is taught in Scripture. Preferential kindness is condemned by John: "He that saith he is in the light, and hateth his brother, is in darkness even until now" (1 John 2:9). "If a man say, I love God, and hateth his brother [neighbor], he is a liar" (1 John 4:20). The remedy is honest self-examination and implementation of the Golden Rule.

With turn-it-off-and-turn-it-on kindness we may gain a reputation of kindness in the community, but those closest to us see our hypocrisy. We compromise their respect and might even earn their bitterness. Scripture warns us, "Provoke not your children to wrath: but bring them up in the nurture and admonition of the Lord" (Eph. 6:4). We often do this out of physical or emotional fatigue or because we are out of synch with God. He can help us to exhibit the love for our children that lies deep within our hearts. He can erase the anger and selfishness that are roadblocks to the nurturing that we want to give our children.

Kindness for attention

"Jason" is not as popular as he would like to be. He hatched an idea to get his classmates to like him. He brought a fistful of one-dollar bills to school and started passing them out to particular people. Word got out that Jason was giving money away, and soon he was surrounded by friends. He gave them each one dollar, but he had a special spot in his heart for "Mindy," so she received two. He glowed in the limelight. But his joy lasted only as long as the money lasted. When his hands were empty, his "friends" disappeared— including Mindy, who gave one of her dollars to "Juan," a boy she wanted to notice her.

When Trishon first met Diniqua, he knew she was the one for him. Diniqua didn't really notice him, so Trishon went out of his way to meet her in the hallways at school, help her with homework, and buy lunch for her. He was consumed with being kind to her, and finally she fell in love with him. They got married and had several children, but Diniqua reflects on those early days and wondered how and when the kindness diminished.

Whether in the realm of romance or not, if we are honest, most of us have to admit that some of our kindnesses are for the attention we receive. We like to impress people. This is deeply ingrained into the human psyche. If we dig deeper, we may find pride at the root of it. We want to make a positive impression; we want to look good. What is so bad about that? Let's look at the big picture again. Yes, a certain degree of this is perfectly natural in romance. But if we are ignoring the "nobodies" of this world and showing kindness *only* to those we want to impress, we are exhibiting the "respect of persons" that James speaks against. The solution is to check our motives and ask, "Am I focusing on the good of others when I am kind, no matter who they are? Am I consistently kind whether or not I receive attention for it? Am I kind to the underdog, like Jesus was?"

Kindness out of fear

Rachel's teacher, Mr. Smith, is skilled at explaining science at the junior high level, and he has high expectations. He also gets angry occasionally. When Rachel and her class- mates have to work with Mr. Smith on extracurricular projects, she is extra helpful and nice to him. She doesn't like him very much, but she is afraid he will become upset otherwise.

I strongly believe in being kind to all people at all times. But sometimes the feelings in my heart toward a few individuals are not kind. I think of these people and a fire burns within me. These were David's reflections in Psalm 39, as he contemplated a difficult situation and difficult people and became increasingly agitated. In my mind, I am arguing with their attitude. I feel my indignation is righteous, of course. Yet when I meet those people I smile and speak nicely. Why? I soften when I see them and realize they are human like me, but part of my motive for kindness is that I am too cowardly to tell them what I am really thinking, for fear of what they might think of me.

This is a very popular form of kindness, though it is hypocritical. Aren't we all guilty? Of course, we shouldn't speak our mind on every occasion; it would serve no good purpose. Kindness out of fear is a restraining force against unkindness. And these kindnesses may be genuine, promoting the well-being of others.

But something is still not quite right. What did David do with his burning thoughts? As he prayed, he meditated on the brevity and vanity of each person's life. Then he placed his hope in God to resolve the situation and to bring peace to his heart. We ought not discontinue the kindness; rather, we ought to bring our thoughts into accord with our actions. If we are honest with ourselves, we have these thoughts because we feel we are better than or at least more right than the other person. So we must swallow our pride and "in lowliness of mind let each esteem other better than [ourselves]" (Phil. 2:3).

Selfish to selfless

Kindness for personal gain, preferential kindness, kindness for attention, and kindness out of fear are all forms of kindness that are mixed with selfishness. When we practice these, we simply don't know the full joy that comes with unselfish kindness. We have to keep track of those to whom we will show kindness. Our conscience bothers us because of our negative thoughts. We are burdened by counting the cost to see if the kindness is worth it. What a lot of trouble!

Kindness out of obedience can be selfish or selfless. It can be grudging or it can be loving. It can stem from a

desire to avoid pain or from a desire for the peace that results from obedience to our Maker.

Kindness from a compassionate heart, kindness because
of the Golden Rule, kindness for the blessing and joy of it,
and kindness because of Christ's kindness to me are forms
of kindness with selfless motives. Selfishness takes a back
seat and selflessness takes over the reins.

When we practice these, we are buoyed above keeping
accounts of giving or withholding kindness. We are free to
show kindness without partiality, without worrying about
whether someone deserves it or not. We are free from the
guilt of hypocrisy. Best of all, we can experience the joy that
comes with giving of ourselves without reservation and the
joy of tasting another's joy as if it were our own.

The kindness of Jesus Christ knows no human equiv-
alent. His kindness was purely selfless. There was no sin
mixed in. He is our example.

Kindness out of obedience

When "Johnny" was five, he got pleasure out of making his
little sister "Amanda" cry. He was good at doing it on the
sly. But his mother caught him and disciplined him often
enough that the unkind behavior diminished. He is kind to
Amanda now.

"Henry" and "Henrietta" became Christians in their
thirties when their children were seven and four years old.
Before conversion, all their time, energy, and money went
towards their own enjoyment. After being born again and
becoming involved in a Bible study, they realized God was
directing them to serve others. They volunteered at a crisis
pregnancy center and an inner city mission, and they helped

neighbors whenever the opportunity arose in the course of daily life.

We are not born kind, sweet, and thoughtful. We are born selfish and sinful. Selfishness is useful for survival. A baby cries in order to get his or her needs met. But the sinful part goes beyond survival. We need to be trained to be kind. Some people are more amenable to this training than others, and thus there are varying degrees of kindness. Johnny needed to be trained to be kind to Amanda. Because he learned kindness and obedience at a young age, he internalized these characteristics.

Henry and Henrietta inherited Christ's goodness when they were saved. The Spirit's internal teaching resulted in love to God and His precepts and love to their neighbor. In turn, this motivated them to obey God's command to be kind.

Kindness from a compassionate heart

A man on his way to Jericho was robbed, beaten, and left for dead. A priest came by but passed by on the other side of the road. So did a Levite. A Samaritan, despised in that culture, came along and showed compassion to the wounded man. He dressed his wounds and then he took him to an inn with instructions for his care and a promise to come back and pay the bill (Luke 10:30–37).

Edna "Sue" Smith lost her two children, five-year-old Ashley and three-year-old Joshua, at the hands of her ex-husband, Patrick Gleeson. He also murdered his girlfriend, Dena Fuglseth. From a charity fund set up in her children's memory, Ms. Smith has made donations to children's organizations in her hometown of Dwight,

Illinois. She also came to Holland, Michigan, to make $1,000 donations to the schools that Ms. Fuglseth's two children attend. She felt that those children's loss of their mother might have been overlooked in all the attention focused on her own children.[1]

It had been a normal church service when a homeless man entered the front of the sanctuary and ambled up the aisle. He was almost to the back when "Juanita" jumped up, grabbed his arm and said, "You've got to hear this." She sat him down between her brother and herself. The minister, seeing what had happened, altered the sermon to present the gospel to the man (in case he left soon) and to the whole congregation.

Christopher Colin, 15, lived in Fort Smith, Arkansas with his thirteen-year-old brother, Nic; nine-year-old sister, Astarte; and their mother, Mrs. Sally Colin. He supplemented his mother's public assistance checks with the $20 he made each week at a convenience store. Christopher would take care of his sister and brother and make sure no one picked on the family. "He was a nice guy," Nic said. Some nights he stayed up until nearly dawn holding his mother's hand when she was frightened or depressed. He promised his mother, who was blind since Christopher was two, "Mama, I'll never leave you and I'll always be your eyes." In March, 1995, Christopher was hit by a car and suffered massive head injuries and was declared brain dead. His heart, liver, one cornea, both kidneys, and both lungs were donated to six people around the country. The other cornea was implanted into his mother's eye. As Mrs. Colin gazed at Nic and Astarte in amazement after the surgery, she said of Christopher, "He kept his word."[2]

A friend once mused, "I wonder if there is such a thing as altruism." He had almost concluded it didn't exist—no one can do something for the benefit of another without always looking for some sort of personal gain. I have pondered this from many angles, and I rejoice to conclude, "Yes, by the grace of God, there is altruism! Praise God there is altruism!" Empathy is the ability of one person to share in the emotions and feelings of another. If we never feel another person's feelings or pain, we have no need to go through the pains of being kind. But if we enter into the emotions of our fellow human beings, then their pain becomes ours and we can only rest when we have done everything in our power to relieve that pain. It's the same way with joy. Our joy is magnified when another person's joy is increased. The exhilaration in this kindness cannot be described in words.

There is a difference between compassion and pity. Compassion is "sorrow for the sufferings or trouble of another or others, accompanied by an urge to help."[3] Pity is compassion that "sometimes [connotes] slight contempt because the object is regarded as weak or inferior."[4] Both result in kindness, but compassion is preferable. If we have an air of condescension or superiority about us, it is demeaning to the person we are being kind to, and they will often detect it. Conversely, when we treat others with dignity, valuing them as much as we do ourselves, then our kindness is much more genuine and effective. "Rejoice with them that do rejoice, and weep with those that weep" (Rom. 12:15).

Kindness for the blessing and joy of it

My mother has many motives for being kind, one of which is simply for the sheer joy it affords her. For example, she used to bring homemade bread and soup to ninety-five-year-old Grandma Jean every week during her dying months. Warm soup, warm bread, warm love of family and friends and God—that's what Grandma Jean lived on. My mom spends most of her waking hours serving our family, our church, our school, and whatever mission effort she sets her heart on. I really believe she's addicted to giving.

Mrs. Maxine Cage-Meeks has been involved in her community for nearly fifty years as a teacher, social worker, and volunteer in various organizations. She was born into the family of a sharecropper. Because they had little money, her parents taught her to clean house, can food, and run errands to help people. This instilled in her a sense of responsibility to help people whenever she can. She said, "I love people and through my work, I've found out about a lot of different resources."[5]

Peter Beintema and Peter Euwema have been friends since they were boys. Pete E. worked with Martha at the *Grand Rapids Press*. Pete E. introduced Pete B. to Martha, and they later got married. One of their four children, Matthew, was born with renal failure. At nearly six months of age, he received his first kidney transplant. When he was twelve, he needed another one. Family members were tested, and no suitable match was found. Pete E. asked to be tested. He was a perfect match. At every stage of the testing and even at the time of surgery, he was told that he could still back out. He never hesitated. Today Pete E. is living well with his remaining kidney, and Matt B. is living well with Pete E.'s donated kidney.

It's the domino effect, one way or the other. Focusing on our own possessions makes us want more. When we get more, we hug what we have all the tighter and we keep thinking of "me " and "more." On the other hand, when we focus on others and their needs, we think, "What can I do or give that would help them?" When we give, the rewards are gratitude, another's happiness, and a deep satisfaction that is a byproduct of generosity. It makes us want to give again. "It is more blessed to give than to receive," taught Jesus (Acts 20:35). Even though we ought not give *for* the rewards, rewards do come when we do give. Jesus explains, "Give, and it shall be given unto you; good measure, pressed down, and shaken together, and running over, shall men give into your bosom. For with the same measure that ye mete withal it shall be measured to you again" (Luke 6:38). If we are miserly to others, they will be miserly to us. Likewise, if we are generous to others, they will be generous to us.

Kindness because of the Golden Rule

Payson Jones is a retired telephone company supervisor in Richmond, Virginia. When his children were young, he began writing and illustrating "Penny Tree" stories. The characters in the stories were handicapped animals such as Grumpsniggy, the ill-tempered aardvark; Tink, a mentally-handicapped rabbit; and Mr. Owl, who needed glasses. Mr. Jones was trying to help his daughter cope with having to wear glasses. He also wanted to teach his children to "see people for who they are and not make fun of or look down on somebody for any differences." His eleven books are being published now with the proceeds going to the Association for the Support of Children with Cancer (ASK), an organization for which he volunteers his time.[6]

Mrs. Dorothy Irvin spent thirty-three years working in

the Grand Rapids Public Schools as a teacher and social worker. She diagnosed special needs children and placed them in appropriate settings. Her aim was always to inspire students to fulfill their potential and to give them hope. One boy had been burned in a fire set by his father. He felt he was a nobody. Mrs. Irvin worked with him and got him into a mentorship program. The boy grew up to be a fine citizen in the community. Mrs. Irvin said, "Though they have special needs and disadvantages, they have ability. The families want the same thing for them that you and I want for our kids."[7]

Recently having completed drug and alcohol rehabilitation, broke and unemployed, Gary Field needed a job. But he didn't even have decent clothes to wear to a job interview. Seven years later, after working his way out of poverty, he opened Career Gear. This non-profit organization is funded by donations and provides a suit and shoes for ex-convicts and ex-addicts to make themselves marketable for a job. They also provide group meetings for instruction in budgeting, finding housing, and getting further counseling. Vision testing, some dental care, and a haircut are also provided. Jeffery Mazard said, "Career Gear built up my self image and my confidence level. It changes your behavior, your conduct—even the way you walk."[8]

"Do unto others as you would have them do unto you." Jesus understood our tendency to think about ourselves first; so in one succinct statement, He gave the key that leads to much kindness. Simply walk in another person's moccasins and carry on as you would like to be treated. Empathy is necessary, as is a realistic understanding of ourselves. But Jesus goes further. He follows the Golden Rule with, "for this is the law and the prophets" (Matt. 7:12). Matthew 22:37–40 explains: "Jesus said unto him, Thou shalt love the Lord thy God with all thy heart, and with all thy soul, and with all thy mind. This is the first and great commandment. And the second is like unto it, Thou shalt love thy neighbor as thyself. On these two commandments hang all the law and the prophets." So the sum of our interaction with God and man is to love God the most and to love our neighbor as ourselves. These two commandments are backed up by creation, our consciences, the Ten Commandments, and the inevitable fruits of the gospel.

Kindness in the face of adversity

In her closing remarks of the trial, the young widow said to the murderer of her husband, "Many nights my kids cry themselves to sleep because they miss their daddy. My baby will never know the loving arms of her father. You've done all of this to me and yet I love your soul. I can forgive you for what you've done to me But *my* forgiveness is not enough. You need to seek the forgiveness of the Lord Jesus."

I know a pastor who has had many unkind words spoken about him. The words were like stabbing knives, but the sympathy of Christ in His sufferings encouraged and upheld him through these times. In the years following, this man has had ample opportunities for revenge, had he chosen to take that path. Instead, he has visited these people in the hospital, met them in their grief at funeral homes, privately deterred others from revenge and bitterness, and given gifts to them. He genuinely does not harbor animosity, but instead desires what is best for them. Though some of the hurt lingers, his behavior is guided by Christ's example.

These examples have involved kindness in the face of adversity. They stand out because harshness and violence contrast so sharply with kindness and love. God's children who have been called to suffer have resorted to their only refuge: Jesus Christ. After He has strengthened them in their dark hours, they understand how He endured hardship and returned love and kindness. If they, by the grace of God, can learn from His experience and lay aside their own honor and natural desires, then they follow in His footsteps. Through it, they grow closer to the Lord and they don't carry the burden of bitterness on their backs.

This is the deepest of human Christian kindnesses. It goes beyond all others. It returns good for evil. It makes a person love his or her enemies. Jesus taught us this way: "And if ye do good to them which do good to you, what thank have ye? for sinners also do even the same.... But love your enemies, and do good, and lend, hoping for nothing again" (Luke 6:33, 35b). Such kindness is beyond human reason; it can only come from a supernatural source, the Spirit of God.

Christ's kindness

Jesus Christ has no peer. His kindness was the ultimate kindness. We human beings are sinners and deserve punishment. But Jesus was perfect; He deserved nothing but heaven. And heaven is where He lived until His Father sent Him to this sinful earth to live for thirty-three years. During that time, He was still God, but He became man as well. For the first thirty years, He lived a common life and experienced every kind of struggle that we do, all the while going about His Father's business without sinning.

He was tempted by Satan to sin, but He resisted the temptation. During the last three years, Jesus traversed the land, teaching simple truths in story form and showing kindness to many. He healed the sick. He raised the dead. He showed compassion to the poor. Many people loved and followed Him, but many hated and despised Him as well. This opposition culminated in Jesus' incredible physical and spiritual suffering on the cross and finally ended in His death, in which He bore sin's punishment for all His people. He was kind in His life and in His death. His death is the greatest kindness there ever was. After three days, He arose from the dead, ministered to His followers for forty days, then ascended to heaven where He remains today, praying for His people.

A Christian wants to follow Jesus Christ's example in every sphere of life. What, then, was He like? What was His personality? How did He exemplify kindness? Isaiah prophesied what Jesus would be like: "He shall feed his flock [His people] like a shepherd: he shall gather the lambs with his arm, and carry them in his bosom, and shall gently lead those that are with young" (Isa. 40:11).

Jesus' deeds describe Him in detail—the miracles of healing performed on people who were blind, crippled, and afflicted with disease, and the forgiveness given to sinners who repented. His own words describe Him further: "Learn of me; for I am meek and lowly..." (Matt. 11:29). "If I then, your Lord and Master, have washed your feet; ye also ought to wash one another's feet" (John 13:14). "For whether is greater, he that sitteth at meat, or he that serveth? Is not he that sitteth at meat? But I am among you as he that serveth" (Luke 22:27).

Jesus compares His Father's compassion to the shepherd who has lost one of his one hundred sheep. He searches the mountains for the wandering one until he finds it. He summarizes by saying, "Even so it is not the will of your Father which is in heaven, that one of these little ones should perish" (Matt. 18:14). His attitude is one of incomparable compassion for sinners.

Mere words cannot capsulize the loveliness of Jesus Christ. Why doesn't everybody love Him? To know Him is to love Him. It can only be that those who don't love Him really don't know Him. Do *you* know Him? Do you love Him? Do you strive to follow His example of kindness?

---

1. "Mother of slain children gives memorials to schools," *Grand Rapids Press*, February 26, 2003, A13.

2. "Her right hand man in life offers Mom sight in death," *Grand Rapids Press*, March 24, 1995, A7. "Mom's sight is final gift from son," *Grand Rapids Press*, March 25, 1995, A5.

3. David B. Guralnik, ed., *Webster's New World Dictionary of the American Language*, Second Edition (Cleveland, Ohio: William Collins Publishers, Inc., 1980), 289.

4. Ibid., 1086.

5. Jodi Burck, "Maxine Cage-Meeks, W.W. Plummer Humanitarian Award," *Grand Rapids Press*, January 26, 2003, J4.

6. Hank Kurz Jr., "Retiree donates his stories to cancer group," *Grand Rapids Press*, February 2, 2003, J3.

7. Elizabeth Slowik, "Dorothy Irvin, Raymond Tardy Community Service Award," *Grand Rapids Press*, January 26, 2003, J5.

8. Alex Polier, "Charity helps men suit up for second chance," *Grand Rapids Press*, March 2, 2003, B12.

PART 2
Kindness Learned

CHAPTER 4
The Kind Wife

Jesus Christ is the foundation of kindness. Families are built on the framework of Jesus' relationship with his Father and with the church on earth. Christ is typified as the bridegroom and the church as His bride. The tender lovingkindness between them is to be emulated in earthly marriages. Love and kindness between husband and wife, in turn, serves to model love and kindness to children. This chapter and the next focus on kindness in marriage.

Kindness happens naturally in a dating relationship. Two people revel in each other's presence. Their aim is to please each other. Unkindness is unthinkable. The motive may be to gain his or her devotion or to express the profusion of love that overflows the heart or both. The first season of marriage is usually spiced with effortless love and kindness as well. In some cases, intruding issues begin to gnaw away at the integrity of a marriage: the drudgery of daily life replaces the excitement of romance, faults in one's spouse become more apparent, one or both partners hold onto grievances, and the arrival of babies brings countless stresses. The tendency of human nature is to slack off from treating each other like a king or a queen. But a vital, growing marriage that will endure through the decades requires self-denial and effort.

God has been very kind in giving me a husband whose fervor of love has not diminished in eighteen years. Joe still expresses his love to me countless times a day with his words and actions. He knows my faults very well, yet he chooses not to call them to remembrance. He appreciates every little thing I do for him. He is a strong, Christian leader in our home, and he makes it easy for me to love and respect him.

Not all men are the same, nor would the women of this world want them to be. What's good for Mary might not be good for Matilda. The husband of "Missing My Mate In Arizona" was cut from a slightly different bolt of cloth than my Joe.[1]

Dear Abby,

PHOOEY on that word "love." Seventy years ago, when I was in my early 20's, I was engaged to a man who swore he loved me with all his heart. He did— until I became very sick. That was the end of our wedding plans.

Years later, I met a man I thought was interested in a mutual friend. I was shocked when he invited me to dinner and a movie. During dinner he said, "I'm not an articulate person." "That's OK," I flippantly replied. "Neither am I!"

We saw each other often after that and time seemed to fly. Then I had an attack of pain that came without warning. My doctor advised immediate surgery. When I told my friend, he listened, then put his hands on my shoulders. In a voice choked with tears, he said, "I *like* you. Will you marry me?" I was so astonished I couldn't speak, for we hadn't even kissed, as unbelievable as that seems.

"You do *like* me, don't you?" he asked anxiously. "Yes," I whispered. I got no further, because I was stopped by our first kiss.

I'm a widow now, and more than 90 years old, nearing the end of my life's journey. Please tell "Feeling Hurt" that a happy marriage can be built on two people "liking each other" at the start. My husband of almost 50 years didn't say love a dozen times, but by his actions, faithfulness, consideration and dozens of ways, he proved—not only to me, but also to the world—he did.

Now I only want to be with him.

Love can be expressed in so many different ways by so many different personalities, but it's the everyday kindness, thoughtfulness, and faithfulness that has the lasting impact. The kind spouse can be quiet or expressive, introverted or extroverted. Kindness may be shown through words or deeds or nonverbal expressions.

There are many acts of kindness to which both husbands and wives are called, like being honest and faithful, helping each other, and speaking with kindness. But due to our physical, emotional, and mental makeup, there are also differences in our expression of kindness and in the kindness we love to receive. As a wife, I describe here the ways we wives can best extend kindness to our husbands. In the next chapter, my husband explains how husbands can best show kindness to their wives.

The wife's call to kindness

It all began so beautifully in the Garden of Eden. Adam

was the crown of creation, made in God's own image. But he was alone. So God made him a lovely wife, Eve. Adam was the head of the relationship, and Eve was his helpmeet. Together they were complete. Their relationship with each other and with God was perfect.

Sadly, they allowed sin to enter their lives early on—Eve first, then Adam. So much changed. Their relationship and covenant with God was severed. Eve would have much difficulty with bearing children, and she would need to submit to her husband. Adam would have to work in the sweat of his brow. And sin would never leave them. A pallor of sadness fell over their lives. The consequences remain to this day.

But Christ came to redeem sinners and, in so doing, He has also redeemed marriage. Marriage, when it is good, is a jewel left over from Paradise. It can be truly and profoundly good when both partners know the Lord Jesus Christ and are walking in His Word. God is so gracious to afford us this lofty joy that can be found in marriage. With His power and strength, we can be the kind, loving spouses God wants us to be. Through Christ, we have access to this joy by praying to and depending on Him.

The role of the wife is clearly defined in Scripture. We learn from Genesis 2 that the "woman was created *after* man, *from* man, *for* the man, and for a purpose—to *help* him."[2] As a wife, I am not only to submit to my husband, but also to respect and reverence him (Eph. 5:22–33). He, in turn, must submit to Jesus Christ. God is not devaluing women with this command. It is a difference in position and function. Every organization or business has a structure of leadership; someone has to lead and someone has to assist and follow.

Each team member is important. It is the same in marriage: husband and wife complement each other.

God not only commanded us to follow this model, He equipped us for it as well. The man is usually bigger and physically stronger, he thinks in a more logical way, and he is more prone to take charge. His inner need is to be respected. The woman is usually smaller and physically weaker, she is more emotional, and she tends to be more nurturing. Her inner need is to be loved. Together, they are a team that gives each other much joy and fulfillment and that accomplishes the task of running their family.

Both are positions of honor. Leadership carries the weight of great responsibility, to the extent that the husband is called to be willing to lay his life down for his wife and family. He must work hard to provide for his family. A wife's position is so important that her husband and their family are incomplete without her. She serves and cares for him and the family in numerous ways.

The strong emphasis that Scripture puts on the husband-wife relationship teaches us that this relationship takes priority over the mother-child relationship. "They two shall be one flesh" (Eph. 5:31). The Christ-church model for marriage teaches a wholehearted devotion to each other. The description in Proverbs 31 of the godly wife focuses first on her doing her husband "good and not evil all the days of her life." Together, husband and wife are the unit that teaches, nurtures, and molds the children.

When we, as wives, embrace this God-given model for marriage, we are halfway to the destination of marital happiness because we are content in our position. Our calling of being kind to our husbands becomes much easier.

Service is the theme of our lives. There is deep joy to be experienced in the act of serving from the heart. But the joy doesn't stop there; the Lord is so kind that He rewards us with love and honor from our families and others.

Hands-on kindness

A beautiful oil painting is made up of thousands of small brush strokes. Similarly, the small acts of kindness that we wives carry out are the brush strokes that help make a beautiful marriage. Below are some practical ways we can instill kindness into our marriages. Our hearts must be in line with God and Scripture, of course; otherwise, our acts will be hollow and lacking in love, and we won't persevere in kindness. Even while walking with God, we need self-discipline to fight our sins and to do His will day by day. Prayer is the means by which we obtain this. God is kind and the giver of kindness.

Do your work

That sounds so unromantic. But the smooth functioning of home is like a basic cake. The frosting comes later, but you first have to have something to put the frosting on. The Proverbs 31 woman is an excellent, though daunting, example. Her husband trusts her to feed and clothe him and the family, to manage the household, and to do all this with pure intentions to benefit them (vv. 11–15, 21–23, 27). She is diligent (vv. 15, 17–19, 27). She buys land and plants a garden (v. 16). She manufactures goods and sells them (v. 24). She helps others who are poor and needy (v. 20).

These are all things she does with her hands. But her character traits are what really make her virtuous. She is strong (v. 25), honorable (v. 25), wise (v. 26), kind (v. 26), and God-fearing (v. 30). She receives honor not only from her husband and children, but also from the people of her city (vv. 28–31).

It is overwhelming to consider her example. But the Lord intends for us to follow the tenor of it. It is kind to wash our husbands' clothes. It is kind to make our homes comfortable and clean. It is kind to fulfill our duties at home so that our husbands can work at their jobs, knowing they can trust us to get the work done. And it is kind for us to fulfill these duties with love.

The most loving thing we can do is to pray for our husbands. The honor and love he feels and the love and humility we receive from this act alone make it indispensable to a vital marriage. But when God's power is added into the mix, we can expect wonderful things. God tells us to pray without ceasing; I find that praying for my husband's cares while I'm doing mundane household chores can be very enriching. It makes him melt, especially if he is grappling with some challenges, and I am drawn more to Joe and to God.

Aim to please him

This one may make the hackles of the feminist rise, and most of us are not immune to her influence. But the wise woman who chooses not to pluck down her house but rather to build it up (Prov. 14:1), will also build up her husband. It's included in loving and respecting him. It flows from the law of kindness in our hearts. Cook him his favorite meals. Smile at him. Say "hello" and "good-bye" with a kiss and a hug. Be affectionate. Forgive and forget. Let him wear the clothes he wants (within reason). Let him rest when he comes home from work. Don't interfere with his hobbies (within reason). Let your home be a haven of rest.

Your words have power; use them wisely. Speak with honor about your husband to your children and to others. Follow his leadership. Show respect and submission to him with words and nonverbal behavior, especially with the tone of your voice. Don't ever belittle him in front of others or in his absence, especially with mockery. Don't control his every action with nagging. You don't want to be like the contentious woman in Proverbs 27:15, who is like a "continual dropping on a very rainy day." Don't blame him for your own problems. Share your own concerns in a loving manner, but don't think of him only as your personal customer service representative. Be cheerful. Praise him. Thank him for working hard and for anything else that deserves thanks—even small things, and even when they are his duty. (Isn't that what we desire?) Show appreciation for his character traits. Ask him how his day was. Be interested in his work, his dreams, and his goals. Listen to him. It is the nature of a man to blossom with this treatment. Treat him like your king, and he'll treat you like his queen.

Keep the romance alive
Start by being best friends. Keep the lines of communication open; converse the way you did when you were dating. Be playful at times. Go on dates on a regular basis and talk about positive, constructive things. Go to a hotel for a night if you can afford it. Flirt with him (and only him). Hug him, kiss him, or pat him as he walks by. Give him backrubs.

Make him feel like a million bucks. Compliment him for his appearance and his character traits. Say "I love you" often.

Ladies, try with all your might to keep up your physical appearance. There are seasons of life when we might not feel so pretty, and having babies and age certainly take their toll. Great self-discipline might be needed, but the dividends are worth it. A vital marital relationship, encompassing physical and emotional aspects, will deter temptation and enrich your marriage.

As challenging as it is, make it a priority to get enough rest. Be nice to yourself: sleep. Getting enough rest keeps you cheerful and more likely to be ready for sexual intimacy. He likes to crown an exhausting day by loving you, while you need to reserve some strength for it. A nurtured relationship results in a healthy, well-rounded relationship. Keep in mind that men and women look at intimacy from opposite sides. We women think like this: "I feel emotionally close to my husband right now; *therefore*, I want to be intimate." Men think, "I want to be intimate right now *in order* to feel close to her." If you understand this difference, you are less likely to jump to an inaccurate conclusion about your spouse's thought patterns and motives.

Our emotional nature as women is both our strength and our weakness. We care deeply about our families, we nurture our children, we multitask quite well, and our radars usually tell us where each child is. But all these skills can cause us to overload ourselves physically and emotionally. The "soccer mom" syndrome is real; we find ourselves frazzled with busyness. The danger is that we are so focused on our children that we gradually whittle our husbands out of the family picture. It can happen insidiously. Before we realize it, we are an emotionally detached couple, and that is fertile ground for temptation. "An ounce of prevention is worth a pound of cure"—this old adage is great for young couples. Dote on your man. Show him kindness. When the kids are asleep, it's time to focus on him. The kids are safe; put them out of your mind and into the Lord's care, and then nurture your marriage.

Problem resolution

An excellent marriage may be a jewel out of Paradise, but an unhappy marriage can be torture. We are all sinners, and problems do arise. We need to have a method to resolve them. Kindness can't fix everything, but when the law of kindness rules, many difficulties can be ironed out.

Where to find help

The first place to look for a solution is to God. Our words and our will can only be subdued from their sinful nature by God's power. He has promised to help when we ask. His love and His example are our roadmap to peace. Let's lean on Him for wisdom and strength.

The second place to look is inside us. Let's ask these questions and answer honestly. "Do I agree with the biblical pattern for marriage? Am I following it with a willing heart? Do I submit to my husband and respect him? Do I follow the example of the Proverbs 31 woman, to the best of my ability?" If we fall short in this area, we have some homework to do.

I've heard the story so many times, it must be more than an aberration. Numerous women came to a difficult stage in their marriage, and either they realized they were not fulfilling their duty or they just decided to give the biblical mandate a desperate try, but they turned their marriages around! Foresight or hindsight made them realize they were part of the problem. They experienced a transformation when they served their husbands, when they thanked and appreciated them, and when they honored and respected them. Their husbands mysteriously changed for the better!

I heard a story once of a very bitter woman who decided to divorce her husband. She relished his misery so much that she thought, "If I am extra sweet to him during these last few weeks of our marriage, then he will be all the more shocked when he is served the divorce papers." So that is what she decided to do. But the Lord turned her plans upside down. Instead of sealing the end of their marriage, her kindness brought out a kind response from her husband. Their love was revived and their marriage was saved.

What are your expectations?

Attitude. Contentment. Expectation. If we drew a scale, ranging from one to ten, for each of these factors, where would you and I be? And how would that affect our relationship with our husbands? Do we find ourselves complaining? "He doesn't tell me what he's thinking." "His workshop is neat, but he throws his dirty clothes on our bedroom floor." "He used to be a gentleman." "I wish he had a job that paid more." "He doesn't help enough around the house." I wonder if it is part of our feminine sinful nature to focus at times on what we are lacking instead of on our blessings. Negative attitudes can swirl around inside us and make us miserable.

A change in attitude can be just as powerful in a positive way and bring us happiness instead. "Maybe he's quiet because I have batted his ideas down too many times. I'll start showing him that I value his thoughts." "I'll put a hamper right where he dumps his clothes and hope his aim is good." "I'll thank him the next time he opens the door for me and tell him how that makes me feel like his lady." "He works really hard. I'll tell him I really appreciate it. And maybe I'll use coupons more and look for sales." "I'll ask him to help at home for specific jobs at specific times. Then I'll thank him for that and for working so hard at his job."

It is crucial for empathy to color our thoughts and our words. We might just be venting about feeling over-whelmed, and we want him just to listen until the storm passes. But his nature is to fix the problem. He begins to feel his solutions are never good enough, and that he is an inadequate husband. That is devastating for a man. He'll either tune us out, rise up in anger, or feel defeated. It's much kinder for us to understand his thoughts and to express ourselves clearly, without dumping emotional garbage on him.

"Mr. and Mrs. White" were a lovely couple, very prim and proper, godly, personable, generous, and helpful. But Mrs. White "henpecked" her husband a fair amount. The day after he died suddenly of a heart attack, she regretted her decades of criticism, and she wished she could have a chance to do it all over, to show him more love, and to appreciate him more.

A dear friend of ours openly shares with young wives how she used to ask her husband to use the towel to wipe the countertop quickly after washing his hands. It would irritate her to see those water drops. But after he died, she was surprised to find water drops on her counter again, and she could only conclude that she was the one who left them there. But then it was too late to apologize. Be humble and don't sweat the small stuff, she concludes. And enjoy your husband while you have him, foibles and all.

"Chill out," the kids say. "Take it easy," we might say. We wives would do well to heed this advice for the small stuff, and maybe even for some big stuff. Charles Spurgeon advised us to keep our eyes wide open before marriage and half closed after we are married. Does it really matter that your husband is a messy eater? Is it so bad that he is extremely protective of the things related to his hobby? Who cares if his Saturday work shirt is ripped? Maybe he buys too many books, but your criticism might only make him sneaky. Even though most of us are determined to change our spouse, we usually don't change them very much. We just stress ourselves out trying. A friend of ours gave up trying to change her husband, and she testified that she was much more relaxed and her marriage improved. I've seen her look at her husband when he was doing one of his quirky things, and she had a calm, amused, loving look on her face.

Women are famous for their intuition. It comes in handy when we interrogate our children and wring the truth out of them, thereby teaching them integrity. But we can take it too far when we examine our husbands and connect a small action with a global character trait. "He is late for supper because he selfishly cares more about his work than he does about our family." "He's just being nice right now so that I let him go hunting on Saturday with his buddies. He's a flatterer." Sometimes we need to step back and not read too far into his motives, to overlook some behaviors, to look at the big picture and see his overall positive characteristics, and to ignore his human foibles. Sometimes it's best to cut him some slack; major in the majors and minor in the minors.

Harness those hormones

Our nephew was given advice about his relationship with his girlfriend: "Once a month, it's all your fault." Isn't that the truth! Hormones are a force to be contended with. We women can change from being placid and pleasant one day to being cantankerous and catty the next. Our emotions during premenstrual or perimenopausal times can make us feel sad, angry, frustrated, irritable, self-pitying, underprivileged, sensitive, weepy, or quarrelsome. We can be fully cognizant of what is happening and yet feel powerless to change. And those around us suffer the repercussions. Why don't those hormone shifts make us more kind and sweet? We sometimes want to cry out to the Lord with Rebekah in Genesis 25:22, "Why am I thus?"

So what do we do, friends? Prayer should be at the top of the list, especially praying ahead of time against our specific weaknesses. Taking care of our bodies physically, especially at PMS time, helps to a degree: proper nutrition, lots of fluids, extra rest, and guarding ourselves against stress. Knowing when to expect the thunderstorm of emotions prepares us and our families to hang on for the ride. I take herbal supplements that have helped curb my ups and downs. Trying to maintain a sense of humor helps. Why not laugh instead of cry? Look in the mirror and replace the snarl with a grin, even if it's forced. The rest is just gritty self-discipline. If we can tell ourselves to delay saying something unkind until tomorrow, we might not feel the need to say it tomorrow. A controlled tone of voice and volume can temper our words. Even though we are rather self-centered during PMS, we need to tell ourselves to have empathy. Our husbands and children will continue to hear the echo of our words, even if we were just expressing the emotions of the day. Be kind, one to another.

Working together

After we have done all we can do from our side as wives, some problems still remain. What is the kind way to deal with them with your husband? Discuss things with love in your heart. Be calm and not angry, lest you say things you'll regret. Do not inflict pain, or you'll have guilt to deal with as well. Plan your discussion so that you don't nag or whine. Remember to build your house up, not tear it down. Be wise in your approach. Look at the big picture. Remember, he's a great guy overall (I hope!); you just need to talk about this problem. Admit your own faults and apologize. Instead of accusing your husband with an inflammatory "You deserted me!," use words like "I felt embarrassed and alone when you went to chat with your friends and left me by myself." Think about how he receives your words and proceed with kindness.

Forgiveness is foundational to our relationship with God and with our husbands. It is an important mark of grace (Matt. 6:14–15). In 1970, *Love Story*'s motto was "Love means never having to say you're sorry." Unless there are two sinless people in this world who just happen to be married to each other, this statement is simply not true. In fact, its opposite is true. Love means saying you're sorry.

We all sin and we all make mistakes. Without apologies, roadblocks are erected. But if mistakes and sin are confessed and forgiven, the slate is clean and life can go on.

Seventy times seven. That's how many times Jesus said to forgive; in other words, infinitely. Forgiveness demonstrates undeserved kindness. Forgiveness means the transgression is washed away, and is not to be brought up again. Grudges, resentment, and disgust are signs that we have not totally forgiven our husbands. It can be difficult to know someone so well that we can predict when he will do something offensive. But if we have forgiven him, we cannot hold it against him. To store up all these negative feelings inside us will only make us bitter, and that is poison to ourselves and to our marriage. "Ye have not, because ye ask not," is our admonition and our encouragement from James 4:2. Prayer, looking to Christ's example, and self-discipline are our tools to return forgiveness and tender lovingkindness to our mate.

Some of you are in a situation that has deteriorated so far that you are destitute of any love or joy. Jesus' words to the church at Ephesus, who had lost its spiritual first love, is fitting advice for you (Rev. 2:1–5). First, think back to the love you used to have. Second, repent of anything you have done wrong. And third, do the first works, the things you used to do to show love. God blesses obedience. Wait on the Lord and see what He will do.

There is a violation of marriage that God considers so heinous that it can break a marriage. It is adultery. If forgiveness and reconciliation are attained, it is wonderful, and a marriage may even be stronger in spite of the scars. But when adultery is not repented of, God, in His kindness, gives His permission for divorce and remarriage (Matt. 19:9).

Tough love is a form of kindness needed in extreme cases. If a husband is addicted to drugs or alcohol, it is kind to let him suffer the consequences of his behavior, in order to draw him away from this sin. If he is sexually abusing a child, it would be kind to him and especially his victim, to take drastic steps to stop this devastating behavior. If he is physically abusing you, kindness does not require you to stay and be injured. A kind wife does not enable her husband to sin.

Let's end on an encouraging note. If one spouse is a believer and the other an unbeliever, the Scriptures instruct the believer to be faithful and to persevere in the Christian walk. It is very possible that the love that keeps shining through will win over the heart of the unbeliever to Christ. Many couples today are a living testimony of this miracle of grace.

In sum, let us as wives treat our husbands with the law of kindness in our thoughts, our words, and our behavior.

---

1. "Missing My Mate in Arizona," Dear Abby, Universal Press Syndicate, January 9, 2003.

2. Elizabeth George, *A Woman's High Calling* (Eugene, Oregon: Harvest House Publishers, 2001), 126

CHAPTER 5

The Kind Husband

by Joel Beeke – Mary's husband

Most men don't appreciate long chapters and long books on how to behave—especially when it addresses how we ought to treat our wives. "Give it to me straight and succinct," you say.

I hear you. So, here it is. Ephesians 5 presents us with the precept, the pattern, and the practice of this loving-kindness.

The precept

The precept is: "Husbands, love your wives" (Eph. 5:25a). This is a command. In the Bible, *love* is usually a verb, not a noun. It is not motivated primarily by what you feel, but by what you are called to do. It is a matter of the will.

Paul says in 1 Corinthians 13:4 that love is kind. The comprehensiveness of this principle is obvious: We need to treat our wives with kindness—always, and in every area of our marriages—not only in our thoughts and our behavior, but also with our words. The law of kindness is not only for Christian wives, but it must also be in our tongues as husbands.

The pattern

We are to show our wives loving-kindness because we are to treat our wives the way Christ treats His bride, the church. This is what Paul is saying in Ephesians 5:25–29. Here are three ways we are to show our wives loving-kindness:

1. *Absolutely.* Christ gives "Himself" for His bride—His total self (v. 25). He holds nothing back. That is obvious from what He has done (think of Calvary), is doing (think of His constant intercession at the Father's right hand), and what He will do (think of His Second Coming). We, of course, do not merit salvation for ourselves. But in terms of the consistent, absolute giving of loving-kindness, Christ is our mentor. We, too, are to give ourselves to our wives. That is a call to consistent, absolute loving-kindness.

2. *Realistically and purposely.* Christ shows kindness to His bride to sanctify her so that He might present her without spot or wrinkle to His Father (vv. 26–27). Christ realizes that His church is far from perfect; she has many spots and wrinkles. She has numerous shortcomings. So we as husbands are to love our wives as if they were perfect, even when we know they are not. Our call and challenge is not to show consistent loving-kindness to a perfect woman but to model Christ in showing consistent loving-kindness to an imperfect wife who has numerous shortcomings. Our purposeful goal must be to influence our wife to good, hoping that our kind love may remove some of the shortcomings, so that our partners may receive freedom to flourish, basking in our kindness.

3. *Sacrificially.* Christ nourishes and cherishes His bride at His own expense (vv. 28–29). So ought we husbands treat our

wives at our own expense with the care that we treat our own bodies. If you have something in your eye, you don't say to yourself, "I think I'll take care of that tomorrow." You give it immediate, tender care. So we ought to treat our wives, sacrificing, at times, our own time and desires. We must care for, protect, nurture, and respect our wives as we would our own bodies.

Are you showing your wife the exemplary loving-kindness of Christ absolutely, realistically, purposely, and sacrificially? "No," you confess, "that is impossible." You are wrong, my friend. Yes, you will always fall short of the mark of perfection since you are not Christ, but by Christ's grace and His Spirit, you can learn to treat your wife with Christlike loving-kindness.

"OK," you say, "prove it to me. Tell me how."

The practice

Kindness is the fundamental ingredient of a good marriage. Paul instructs Christians in Colossians 3:12 to "put on kindness." We are to adorn ourselves with it at all times and in all situations. Most of marriage is not honeymooning in the Alps or the Caribbean. Most of marriage is made up of small acts of daily kindness, like putting toast in the toaster for your spouse, asking each other how your day went, or sending a silent, warm smile across the room.

Exercising consistent loving-kindness as a husband to your wife involves working at three areas in your marriage: demonstrating kindness, preventing unkindness, and reacting to unkindness.

Demonstrating kindness

There are thousands of ways that we husbands can demon-

strate kindness to our wives every day. Here is a sampling—
add your own to this list!

1. *Show great interest in your wife as a person.* Care about her.
Conversational communication is critical for your wife.
Communicate with her. After church worship or times of
spiritual fellowship ask her what she learned and how her
soul fared. Ask her how her day went and how the kids
were. Ask her about her dreams, fears, and frustrations.
Learn to listen; learn to reflect her feelings back to her so
that she opens up the more. Be her "soundingboard."

2. *Pray for your wife as you pray with her.* Perhaps the kindest and
most valuable thing you can do for anyone is to pray for that
person. John Newton once remarked that his best friends in
the world were those who were lisping his worthless name
each day in the ears of the Lord of Sabbaoth.

After I visited and prayed with a dear elderly parishioner
in the hospital who was in great pain, I remarked before
leaving, "I wish I could do more for you." She rebuked
me. "Pastor," she said, "you've just done more for me than
anything else in the world. You've just brought me in prayer
into the presence of my Savior and commended all my needs
into His almighty hands."

The kindest thing you can do for your wife is to pray for
her in secret and with her. Lay out her needs before God.
Be earnest in pleading for her spiritual growth, for Christ
to meet her daily needs, for relief in physical and emotional
difficulties. Let her feel your strength and your tenderness
at the throne of grace on her behalf.

3. *Love your wife dearly.* Love her as she is. Love her with her
faults. Please her (1 Cor. 7:33). Respect and honor her:

"Likewise, ye husbands, dwell with [your wife] according to knowledge, giving honour unto the wife, as unto the weaker vessel, and as being heirs together of the grace of life" (1 Pet. 3:7).

Treat your wife tenderly. Let your entire demeanor treat her like she is a rare vase rather than like a piece of outdoor patio furniture. Tell her every day how much you love her. Shower her with affection—verbal affection, physical affection, emotional affection, spiritual affection. Seldom walk past her in the home without a hug. Write her an affectionate letter or give her a warm card, expressing your affection. Add a few paragraphs to the card extolling how lovable she is, and give it to her at an opportune private time. It will bring her to tears of joy and appreciation.

Your wife is God's gift to you. Appreciate her. Thank her every day for who she is and for what she gives to you. And give yourself to her (Eph. 5:25). I once read of a Puritan husband who was accused by his pastor of making an idol of his wife because he loved her too much. The poor man went home much troubled, but soon returned to his pastor and said, "I humbly believe that you are wrong, for I read in Ephesians 5:25 that I am to give myself to my wife as Christ did to the church. When I read that, I realized that I still don't love her enough for my giving of myself to her doesn't begin to compare to how Christ gave Himself for me."

4. Heap praise and compliments on her. Tell her how beautiful and wonderful she is. Be intimate, specific, creative, and repetitive in your compliments. Compliment her kindness, her thoughtfulness, her smile, her dress, her hair, and a thousand other things. (I once told my wife that I wanted to tell her 100 things I loved about her. It took nearly

twenty minutes, but it was time well spent!) Compliment
her with affection in your voice, with love in your eyes, and
with arms of embrace.

Tell her what pleases you and then compliment her when
she meets your needs. In areas where she may have faults
or be weak, compliment her when she shows effort and
strength. Rather than criticize her weak times, compliment
her strong times. Stress the positive! Be affirmative and
positive as much as possible without being fake.

Praise her in the presence of others, too, especially your
own children, as the wise husband did for the Proverbs
31 woman (v. 28). Never allow your children to speak dis-
respectfully to her or about her.

The road to the divorce court begins where a husband
stops complimenting his wife. Before long, husband and
wife take each other for granted, immerse themselves in
their own worlds, and become like two ships passing in
the night.

Have you ever noticed how engaged couples compliment
each other all the time? Take a page out of their book.
Marriages seldom fold where both people compliment each
other on a daily basis. In fact, I often tell young couples in
my premarital counseling sessions with them that I have
been counseling people for thirty years but have never yet
had to counsel any couple who were both complimentng
each other on a daily basis about substantial matters.

5. *Learn your wife's language of love.* Aim to please. If she loves
daisies and you love roses, by all means, get her daisies
when you get her flowers. Does she enjoy eating out? If you
can afford it, take her out often. Ask her what restaurant
she wants to go to. Surprise her by taking her out for meals

or desserts when the children aren't around. And don't forget to treat her like a gentleman throughout. Does she appreciate it when you open doors for her? Be sure to do it. Does she appreciate engaging conversation (what woman doesn't)? Don't be looking all around the restaurant and eating your food as if your were alone or with a business partner. Look into her eyes. Speak with your mind and heart to her mind and heart.

Learn to deny yourself. If you and your wife feel differently about something, and you sense that she feels as strong or more strongly about the issue than you do, choose to follow her feelings. Great and kind husbands learn to put God first, their wives second, and themselves third.

6. *Cultivate shared friendship and interests with your wife.* In their *The Intimate Marriage,* Howard and Charlotte Clinebell show that intimate marriages are those in which both husband and wife view each other as best friends and find many common interests.[1]

My wife and I have taken a walk together nearly every day for most of the years of our marriage. This is a great time for both of us. She also usually takes a short bike ride every day. She is a great biker; she has gone on several long-distance bike trips. Biking means nothing to me; in fact, I always thought that I didn't care for it at all. But recently, I decided to join my wife on an early morning bike ride. She was so pleased that it actually made me pleased. Now I've been biking with her quite regularly and am thoroughly enjoying it. After eighteen years of marriage, we've just found a new common interest.

Worshiping God together, walking together, talking together, taking trips together, doing hobbies together, visiting mutual friends together—whatever it may be, the more common interests you develop, usually the better your marriage will be.

Do you desire to be best friends with your wife? Share with her. Share yourself, your faith, your trust, your support, your congeniality, and, above all, your love.

7. *Provide your wife with biblical, tender, clear, servant leadership, not ruthless authoritarianism.* Tragically, many husbands don't understand that wives view their families as an extension of themselves, much as we men view our work as an extension of ourselves. Be the spiritual leader, the father-shepherd, of your wife's children. Lead your family daily in Bible study and prayer. Be the family office-bearer. Be a teaching prophet, a praying priest, and a guiding king. Talk with your wife and children about the truths of God. Pray with them about these truths. Model these truths. When our wives see us lead their children with kind, spiritual leadership, it touches their hearts.

Using Christ as your pattern, learn to show servant leadership to your wife. Delight in serving her, remembering that great leaders are those who learn to serve (Matt. 20:25–26). Share some mundane chores with her. Ask her forgiveness if you have neglected her or lorded yourself over her.

Learn to esteem your wife more than yourself. Nourish and cherish her as Christ does the church and as a man does his own body (Eph. 5:28–29). That will mean, of course, that just as you sometimes must say "no" to the desires of your own flesh, so there will be times you will have to say "no" to your wife's desire. If your wife loves the Lord and you've learned to talk things over in a kind way, those times will be few. But when they do surface, be sure that your wife feels your love in denying her request. She must know that you deeply believe that your "no" is for her best welfare and not a rejection of her as a person. Never say "no" roughly, crudely, or capriciously.

Physically, we are the giants in marriage, but God commands us to be gentle giants. We are to be the head, not the fist. As the head, you have eyes to admire your wife and see her needs, you have ears to listen to her, lips to compliment her and kiss her, and a brain to understand her and think about what matters to her. So if you're the head, act like it; don't act like a fist![2]

Preventing unkindness

1. Never forget the basic physical, mental, spiritual differences between men and women. Physically, your wife is weaker; mentally, she is more emotional; spiritually, she is more affectionate. Read Cecil Osborne's *The Art of Understanding Your Mate.* You'll be glad you did. It will help you understand how male rationalism and female emotionalism can really work effectively together, providing you understand your spouse. God made us to complement each other, not to antagonize each other.

2. Never allow any relationship to take priority over your friendship with your wife. Stay each other's best friends. Share of yourself as you would share with no other. Don't give an undue amount of time to your extended family or friends.

3. Never fail to use the "sandwich principle" when criticizing your wife. I learned this principle from the apostle Paul. Have you ever noticed that nearly every letter Paul wrote to a church was actually aimed to deal with criticisms that he had about that church? Yet, in his letters, Paul does not begin with criticism. He begins (1) with compliments and blessings, (2) then kindly approaches his criticisms of them and provides solutions for their problems, and (3) wraps things up with kind affirmations at the end of his epistle. When the churches felt his love in the opening and closing sections, they would realize that Paul was not criticizing them globally, but was really focusing only on one or a few things. They could then accept his criticisms in the middle section without feeling offended, knowing that in the main Paul cherished them and thought highly of them.

So how does that work toward our wives? Let me show you first how not to do it. Let's say that you have become very weary of your wife being very late in the preparation of your evening dinner meal. If you said to her, "Martha, I'm tired of you never getting these meals ready on time," what kind of response do you think you will get? Mildly put, an unkind one—perhaps something like this: "OK, if that's all you think of my meals, from here on in, you just make your own meals." You were unkind and ungrateful to your dear Martha who has been making your meals every single night, so you have just made a problem (late meals) into a far worse problem (a wife feeling taken for granted). You made your wife feel like she was a total failure.

Here's what you should do. At some opportune moment after the meal, perhaps while you are going for a walk together hand-in-hand, you say something like this: "Martha, you are such a great wife. I love you dearly. You take incredibly good care of me. Thanks for being such a good cook. [Here you are laying down the first slice of bread of the sandwich you are giving Martha—a slice of compliments. Now comes the meat of criticism:] But I was just wondering something. It seems that, quite often lately, when I get home from work about 6:00 p.m., we don't have dinner until about 7:30 p.m. Do you think there's a possibility that we could aim to get your delicious dinners together a tad earlier so that it doesn't negatively impact our evening activities? Perhaps I could help you a bit. After dinner, I feel like we too often have to rush through family worship lately. I hope you understand where I'm coming from, but [here comes the second slice of bread!] don't get me wrong. I love your meals, and you are a great wife."

Martha will eat that sandwich because she will feel your love and won't feel threatened. She'll probably say, "No problem, George. You know, I think you're right. I do seem to be getting later and later. I'll do my best to make the meals earlier. Would 6:30 be all right?"

"That would be wonderful, dear. Thank you so much for understanding."

You have just resolved a problem and prevented unkindness through following the sandwich principle much like Paul did to the churches he wrote.

4. *Never compare your wife unfavorably to other people.* Again, you will make her feel like a failure. Nor should you ever criticize her in any area that it is not possible for her to change. This includes the lack of certain intellectual attributes (such as one's IQ) or physical attributes (such as the shape of her nose). This is simply being mean and only builds internal resentment in your wife. Nor should you bother to criticize trivia.

Be patient with your wife. Don't find fault. Ignore the molehills. Deal only with the mountains.

A fundamental guide for marriage is that you are not going to change your partner all that much anyhow. What you see is what you get. In the long run, husbands who nitpick their wives produce bitter, unhappy spouses who become increasingly unresponsive over the years.

If you are a critical person, learn to criticize yourself rather than your partner. Don't ask, "How can my wife be a better spouse," but "How can I be a better husband?"

5. *Never criticize your wife in the presence of anyone.* Don't use a joke or a half-joke about women in general to slyly put down your wife. Don't criticize her in private in front of your family or your friends. How would you like it if she complained about you to her mother?

Avoid public disagreements. If you disagree with what she said or did in public, approach her kindly in private afterward, always remembering to use the sandwich principle.

6. *Never fail to give your wife an appropriate amount of freedom and "space."* Give your wife sufficient freedom so that she can strive to be a Proverbs 31 woman. Give her space to exercise her own personality in running the household in a God-fearing way.

Don't smother her or her personality. Don't try to micro-manage her or control her purchase of every small item. Provide her, as best you can, with a reasonable budget to work with. Don't tell her how to run her kitchen. Don't control her usage of time.

Respond as soon as you can to her needs in the home,

remembering that a wife views her house as an extension of herself. Fix the broken toilet, have it fixed, or give her the freedom to get it fixed. Don't let it languish. To you, it is just a broken toilet and there is another one in the house that can be used. To your wife, your lack of involvement signals that you don't really care too much about her after all.

Reacting to unkindness

How should we react if our wives are unkind to us?

1. *Never forget the example of Christ,* "who, when he was reviled, reviled not again; when he suffered, he threatened not; but committed himself to him that judgeth righteously" (1 Pet. 2:23). If Christ, who was perfect, endured so much unkind abuse without reviling, how much more shouldn't we, who are usually at least partially guilty, respond to reviling with kindness? Be compassionate, gracious, and patient when your wife is unsympathetic, mean, and impatient, because Christ is compassionate, gracious, and patient toward you when you act far worse towards Him than your wife ever acts towards you.

2. *Never be defensive.* Acknowledge the areas in your life that need improvement. Admit when you are wrong. Remember, you are a sinner. Be quick to say, "I'm sorry," and to ask, "Will you forgive me?"

3. *Never stop being a gentleman.* Be polite, mannerly, and courteous. Don't render evil for evil. Be man enough to control your anger. Don't raise your voice, even if she raises hers.

Hear your wife out, even if she is piling criticism on you thick and heavy without using the sandwich principle. Try to understand where she is coming from. What is she *really* saying? Are her complaints justified? Have you been neglecting her? Or is this just the wrong time of the month?

Whatever the case may be, ride out the storm. Remember, *listening* is usually more important for a woman than *solving*. Later on, when she is sweet and calm again, you can talk about a solution.

Don't forget that women are deeply touched by kindness. If you remain kind in the face of your wife's unkindness, most wives will return to their husbands before nightfall, asking for forgiveness for their unkindness.

4. *Never let the sun go down upon your anger* (Eph. 4:26). Come together again as quickly as possible, even if some issues have not been fully resolved. Read the Scriptures and pray together—lovingly—so that grudges are released.

"Charity is kind" (1 Cor. 13:4). Marriage ought to be the kindest setting in all the world. Such loving-kindness doesn't get envious or proud, it doesn't get provoked easily, and it isn't judgmental. It bears, believes, hopes, and endures all things (1 Cor. 13:4–7). Husbands and wives, "Be ye kind one to another, tenderhearted, forgiving one another, even as God for Christ's sake hath forgiven you" (Eph. 4:32).

---

1. Howard J. Clinebell, Jr. and Charlotte H. Clinebell, *The Intimate Marriage* (New York: Harper & Row, 1970).

2. I am indebted to Geoff Thomas for the head-fist analogy and the thoughts in this paragraph.

CHAPTER 6
Parenting with Kindness

The nature vs. nurture debate is still alive. Are children born as blank slates and molded solely by their environment? Or are they destined to manifest whatever personality they have at birth? If nurture were the only determining factor, all the children in each family would turn out much the same. If nature prevailed, children would become exactly and only what they were when they were young. Both nature and nurture exert their forces on a child, molding and shaping him during childhood, especially during the early years. Any parent of two or more children can testify that each child has a unique personality, sometimes evident before birth. And all parents can see the results of their parenting, whether good or bad, reflected in the behavior of their children. Dr. James Dobson visits this debate in a fresh and detailed way in his book *The New Strong-Willed Child.*[1]

Unfortunately, mainstream psychology has adhered more closely to the blank-slate viewpoint, while mainstream childrearing approaches have led parents down the path of permissive parenting. What is the result of this combination? Bewildered and weak parents. These philosophies are contradictory. On one hand, the blank-slate approach implies the child needs to be molded; that slate needs someone to write on it. On the other hand, the permissive approach to childrearing leads parents to believe that the goodness of their children's hearts will come shining through if they will only let Johnnie and Susie be who they want to be. And what is the result? It's a battle between spoiled, demanding children and frustrated, angry parents. Johnnie and Susie emerge being who they want to be, but not what their parents had hoped for. It is likely they will not fully respect their parents because Mom and Dad were not strong enough to earn it. Their love for their parents might ebb and flow with the benefits received. They will go through life focused on "what's in it for me?" rather than "what can I do for you?"

There has to be a better philosophy than this depressing combination. We can be thankful that we are not left to our own understanding for this monumental task of childrearing. The timeless Scriptures are full of wisdom. Our culture has changed since the Bible was written, but human nature remains the same.

A philosophy of kindness

The most effective parenting takes place when the child's whole environment is consistent. If kindness is to be taught in the home, both Dad and Mom, or a single parent alone, must value its importance. As parents, our philosophy of life must be laced with kindness. From our philosophy flows our behavior. The biblical foundation is love to God above all and love to our neighbor as ourselves. A humble servant's heart is necessary. Proverbs 31:26 describes the virtuous woman: "in her tongue is the law of kindness." It is not only the mother who is to be kind, though she has great impact on the atmosphere and daily running of the home. In combination with a father's kind leadership, the effect of kindness will permeate the entire family.

Marinated

The wonderful thing about marinated chicken is that the flavor is not confined to the surface but is infused throughout the meat. Through the hours of soaking, spices have seeped into the center. The vinegar tenderizes the meat and the oil moisturizes it so that, when the heat is applied, the chicken cooks but doesn't get dry. A philosophy of kindness in a family will do the same thing. When a husband shows love to his wife and a wife shows respect to her husband as the Bible teaches, peace and joy are more likely to occur, and the heat of the trials of life can be handled better. The children observe the kindness exchanged between Mom and Dad and are more prone to follow their example. Parents who treat their children with dignity and kindness will be the beneficiaries of it as well. Insisting on kindness between siblings may take years to bear fruit, but perseverance will pay off eventually. Speaking well of our neighbor at the dinner table, especially those who are underprivileged or shunned, will engender kindness to that person when our child meets him or her in public. By doing charity work as a family, we teach our children that every human being has worth and dignity. Kindness to animals and the environment will promote a lifelong care of God's creation.

These are worthy ideals at which to aim. They add flavor to life. It is God's will to pass on a legacy of kindness. Yet our best efforts will fall short without the Lord's blessing.

Prayer and searching God's Word are part of the marinade. Without them, life is tough, dry, and flavorless.

Inconsistent kindness

An inconsistent philosophy of kindness may work for a while, but in time the façade will begin to crack. If we choose the kindness-coated-but-not-infused method, our children may adopt the same philosophy. They observe our behavior in public and in private, and they compare the two. If they see a discrepancy, the result is unpredictable and often not pretty. Samantha observes her parents speaking nicely to Mr. and Mrs. Jones at the school music night, but hears them saying on the way home, "Did you notice Mrs. Jones's clothes were dirty, and that Mr. Jones smelled like he hasn't showered in weeks?" On the playground the following day, Jason Jones runs into Samantha and she blurts out, "Don't touch me! You guys are dirty!" Jason is hurt and tearfully tells his parents what happened. The cycle of pain and rejection has begun in one family, and the cycle of pride and superiority continues in the other. And kindness is not in the mix. If our philosophy practices "kindness when we feel like it," our own reputation will bear it out. Then our children will build a reputation of their own of favoritism and unkindness. But worse, God is not honored nor loved and neither is our neighbor.

Without a principle of kindness in our hearts, we tend to allow familiarity to breed contempt. We act nice in public because we want to preserve our reputation, but we are irritable and cruelly honest at home, hurting those we really love the most. We take our loved ones for granted, and we take our frustrations out on them without restraint.

Sadly, it often takes serious injury or death to realize how precious our family members are.

Love and affection

Our children must feel our love and affection. As parents, we need to express it in words and actions. The manner in which we display our love changes with the age of our children, but affection is life-long. Start young and never stop. Did you ever wonder why babies and toddlers are so cute? I am convinced part of the reason is so that we fall hopelessly in love with our children. When our children were young, and my love batteries needed recharging, I would just go look at sleeping Calvin, Esther, or Lydia. There is nothing more beautiful than a sleeping baby. I still occasionally peek at them when they are sleeping, and I feel that love all over again. So often in our busy lives we forget to count our blessings and think about how dear our children really are to us. We need to take time to meditate on the gifts God has given us.

From the thoughts flow the words and actions. You can't say, "I love you!" too much. It is a good thing to get used to. If you don't get in the habit of it at a young age, it will be very difficult to say even when you really want to. Let your hugs and kisses and cuddling flow as well.

Children need physical contact and affection from their parents to grow attached to them. Studies of children lacking affection during their first years have shown that aberrant behavior often results. These children are "often pleasant and affectionate on the surface, indeed indiscriminately affectionate, but seemingly indifferent underneath; lacking pride; and displaying incorrigible behavior problems that often included sexual aggressiveness, fantastic lying, stealing, temper tantrums, immature or infantile demands, and failure to make meaningful friendships."[2]

Children need the security of knowing that we love them and that we will always be there for them. I read of a man's description of his mother, and one thing that stood out in his memory was that, every time his mother looked at him, she "brightened." Let's make a more conscious effort to smile. It should be simple. A smile chases away the shadows in the heart of both the giver and the receiver, and it smoothes out the worries of a child's heart. Let's not let the drudgery of everyday life overshadow the abundance of blessings we enjoy. Count those blessings and give an extra hug and a kiss, a comment of affirmation, and big smiles to your child every day.

Foundational principles

Parents must agree on a philosophy for childrearing in general and teaching kindness in particular. Ideally, a dating couple should discuss these issues in depth before they enter marriage and bring children into the world. Our tendency is to follow our parents' techniques and assume our spouse will do the same (follow *our* parents, that is). Things go much more smoothly if we are mentally prepared before the baby comes and if we have come to an agreement before stressful situations arise.

Expectant parents often do everything they can think of to physically prepare for the arrival of their little one. But when Junior makes his grand entrance and does not behave according to the book, and Mom is battling the balance of hormones, and Dad is supposed to be stable but isn't, all that preparation flies out the window! This is just the beginning. Throughout the whole experience of childrearing, there are moments of impasse, disagreement, confusion, and frustration.

A place of refuge

We need a place to go. Scripture is the answer. God has promised to lead us if we study the pages of His Word and pray for His guidance. Of course, the Bible won't tell us how often to feed Junior during the night, but it will advise us to seek the advice of wise counselors (Prov. 11:14), and it will tell us to pray and find peace with God for the short and long term (1 Pet. 5:7). The Bible won't tell us how many minutes Junior should spend on the computer, but it will tell us that we should focus our minds on whatever is good and pure (Phil. 4:8). There simply has to be a place where we agree to meet, a place that promises the final word of wisdom. Only in the Bible can we comfortably acquiesce to the wisdom of the One whom both parents agree to follow.

Our children need a place of refuge, too. Since parents represent God to a young child, that safe place is parents in the home. Children need to know we are there for them. It is biblical for the mother to be a "keeper at home" (Titus 2:5). It is kind for her to be a consistent presence there, to be available as much as possible. That's why I have supplied an appendix on the value of a mother's staying at home, along with encouragements and methods to make it work.

Born sinners

Scripture teaches that our children are born as sinners (Ps. 51:5; Rom. 3:8–20 and 5:12–19). Reality bears it out early in the child's life, as demonstrated by the angry cry of an infant who doesn't want to leave her mother's warm arms for a lonely crib, or the biting and jabbing toddler who is stealing his friend's toy. If we as parents don't believe original sin exists, we are in for a long and arduous journey of childrearing. We won't be able to understand why our little darling is not blossoming under our love but seems to despise us instead. If we do believe children are sinners, we are more realistically prepared for this journey. Knowing our children are sinners does not minimize our love for them. Rather, we realize they inherited their sin from us and we all need to be redeemed by Jesus Christ. We expect a battle when good and evil clash, but the armor of God helps us (Eph. 6:11–20). We have compassion with our children's failings and work with them to grow and learn.

Discipline

Discipline is necessary. It may not seem kind, but it really is. A barbed wire fence may seem to be a cruel thing with which to surround a beautiful free-spirited horse, but some friends of ours wish their fence had not broken when their son's beloved horse got free one night, wandered into the road, and was hit by a car, killing both the horse and the driver. If we agree our children are sinners, then discipline is needed to root out that sin. Solomon, the wisest man, wrote in the Proverbs that discipline is a sign of love (13:24), offers hope for lifetime habits (19:18), drives foolishness from the child's heart (22:15), will give the child wisdom (29:15), will give the parents rest and delight instead of shame (29:15, 17), and will even deliver the child's soul from hell (23:14). Paul cautions us to control discipline by urging us not to provoke our children to wrath, but to nurture and admonish them, lest they become discouraged (Eph. 6:4, Col. 3:21). I defer to Dr. Dobson's wisdom and biblical treatment of the subject of corporal punishment.[3] In short, God tells us to use corporal punishment with great love and discretion, and He tells us that it works.

If there is one aspect of discipline that sets the scene for all others, it is squelching defiance the first moment it occurs, as well as every time it resurfaces. If parents pick one battle to win, it must be this one. If they win, life will be much easier; if they lose, they will have a difficult journey. Having been a teacher before being a parent, and seeing how difficult it was to control a defiant twelve-year-old, I determined I would nip this character trait in the bud in our own children. My own pride (and perhaps my own defiance) was useful, because when faced with a child's defiance, my feeling was, "How dare you speak to me in that tone?" As I look back, I remember my dad having zero tolerance for defiance. Parents must strongly support each other in this area. "You will not speak to Mommy in that way. It's not respectful. Let's say it differently."

If we could crawl into our toddler's mind, we would see he has his own agenda, and selfish desires are quite likely at the center of it. The sooner we can write, "Dad and Mom are in charge because God put them there" on his heart, the sooner we get on with the business of molding his strengths so that his life is God-directed, not self-directed. Deal with defiance quickly and decisively.

The enemy in your home

In order to remove a stain, we would not lay a white shirt

out on a muddy table. Likewise, it is counterproductive to allow influences into our home that go directly contrary to our instruction. If we don't want our little boys to beat up animals or their sisters, why would we allow them to play a violent video game? If we don't want our daughters to become sexually promiscuous, why would we allow them to watch TV shows that promote a sensual view of life? It's akin to taking the down escalator to get upstairs. We must take charge! Let's remove the influences—I'm talking mostly about media influences—so that we don't have to compete with the powers of evil that aim to capture the hearts and souls of our precious children. If the TV were a person who performed each program live, we would never invite him into our home, especially not to babysit our children. Just because entertainment is interwoven into our society does not mean it is good, nor does it mean we have to partake of it without discretion. It only makes sense to saturate our homes with influences that go hand-in-hand with the principles of Christian living.

Serving others

Another principle that rounds out a Christian home of kindness is serving others. This is not optional. Serving must be woven into the very fabric of our family life. It ought to be as natural as eating and drinking. The variety of service work a family can do is limited only by their imagination. The whole world lies open as an opportunity for singles and married couples with no children. There are seasons of family life when the amount of serving we can do is curtailed. But even during the busy seasons, we can fit it in with our daily work.

An example is preparing a double portion of supper and delivering it to a family that has a member in the hospital. My brother and his wife have "adopted" an elderly woman. They fix plates of leftovers, freeze them, and bring them to Katherine the next time they visit her. Then it is easy for her to have a warm meal at her convenience. Henry and Teresa's children go along to check on Katherine and help with odd jobs.

When children are elementary-school age, they can help out with neighborhood, church, and school projects. Opportunities abound for teens to serve, from hospital volunteering to raking leaves to mission trips. Serving others "along the way" can be done anytime, any place. Simply open a door for someone, or let someone into your lane. Speak kindly to a homeless person when you encounter one. Setting an example of kindness for our children is not wasted effort. Random acts of kindness are wonderful, but a purposeful life of serving is better.

Purposeful teaching

Setting an example of thoroughgoing kindness is essential. So is clear instruction in the ways of kindness. It all begins at home. Children are able to exhibit unkindness at an early age; that is the time purposefully to begin teaching kindness. When our children were young and would show unkind behavior to each other, I would separate them from each other and stop the action with a firm, repeated, and (I hope) calm "no" or "stop." Then we would determine what had happened and where the blame lay. Whoever was guilty had to say "I am sorry," and the other one had to say "I forgive you." Sometimes it went both ways. If the situation called for it, we would replay the scene with a more congenial course of action. We would discuss it, administer discipline when necessary, and end with a prayer and a hug. Whenever I controlled my own irritation at the offending child and reminded myself that this was a teaching opportunity, this practice worked well.

Confession and forgiveness

I have spoken to parents before who do not believe in requiring their children to say "I am sorry" or "I forgive you" because the children don't sincerely mean it. I believe that few children will come to this point naturally, but they need to be nurtured in that direction. We teach our children to share their possessions with others, whether or not it is sincere. We don't allow them to steal or hit, even though they sincerely desire to do so. Sincerity is not the standard. If we wait for sincerity, without directing them, we will simply end up with a sincere sinner. In order to teach our children emotions of humility and compassion, we must first mold their behavior, since that is what their young minds comprehend. Then we mold their minds to empathize with others and to show enough love to promote the good of others. This takes time.

As parents, we must also apologize to our children. Joe and I have done this since Calvin, Esther, and Lydia were very young. We seek their forgiveness when we have overreacted, for example, and hurt our children's feelings or wrongly accused them. They are very willing to forgive, and it clears the air and gets us back on a loving track. At the time of this writing, our children (ages 16, 15, and 11) are willing to volunteer their wrongdoings to us. I wonder if there is a connection between our willingness to admit wrong and theirs. I hope and pray it continues, by God's grace.

Confession and forgiveness are at the very center of our relationships with our neighbor and with God. We all need to apologize in order to have healthy relationships. And unless we want to send ourselves to the grave early by housing bitterness in our hearts, we had better learn to forgive. By teaching these habits to children, we not only lubricate the machinery of human interaction; more importantly, we set a framework that can be of great assistance in a saving relationship with God. If a person has a difficult time saying "I am sorry" to a relative or friend, how much more difficult it will be to express the same feelings to God! And if we can't forgive others, we will encounter a roadblock when we need to receive God's forgiveness.

The first kindness

In the busyness of daily life, it is easy to forget that our children have eternal souls. We have to prepare them for adult life, but first and foremost, we must do everything in our power to prepare them for eternity. That includes earnestly teaching them the truths of Scripture, bringing them to church, discussing the sermons, engaging in family worship, counseling them about their personal spiritual life, warning them of sin, presenting the gospel lovingly, teaching them about God's gracious covenant, and representing God's character with ours.[4] Behind the scenes, we must be on our knees, storming the throne of grace for God to work with His almighty Spirit in their souls. We can die young or old. It is kindness to train our children in the pathways of Jehovah.

"No!"

I once met a mom who said, "I try to say 'no' to my daughter as little as possible." I have mulled that one over many times. I would agree it's a worthy ideal, and I have tried to become more positive with my children. But I would accompany it with a caution, "Don't hesitate to say 'no' when you need to!" Again, our children are sinners. If a friend were taking a path through the woods that led by the domain of a poisonous snake, you would urgently tell her, "No! Don't go that way!" Why then should we hesitate to tell our children not to go down a dangerous path? It is kindness to tell children "no" when what they are doing is not good for them, especially if it could have eternal consequences.

Self-discipline

The transition from being a playing child to a working adult happens gradually over approximately eighteen years. For the naturally industrious child, this is a pleasurable journey. Children who would much rather play all day than work, may encounter a few more obstacles. A parent who does not teach his or her child to work in an age-appropriate way is not showing kindness but is setting the child up for failure and misery. Our children may complain, pout, shout, or cry when we make them work, but it simply must be done. The child's will to do negative things must be broken.

When children accept work as a part of life, they are on their way to contentedness. The irony about self-discipline is that by aggressively doing what we don't want to do, we gain a sense of accomplishment when the job is done. The next time it becomes a bit easier, and before long we enjoy the satisfaction so much that we actually enjoy the work. Our children must be realistically prepared for adulthood, and they probably won't catch on simply by watching us. They need to be active participants, and the younger we start with age-appropriate tasks, the sooner they will learn that work is a normal part of life and can be enjoyable. It is kindness to our children (and to their future spouse and employers) to teach them to work well.

I once heard it said that every day we should do one thing that we don't like to do. I mentioned this to a friend and he replied, "I do, I get up in the morning." There are many tasks that make up our daily routine that we don't naturally like. By "naturally," I mean our original attitude to that task before it became routine. Therefore, the younger our children are when we ingrain routine tasks in them the better. As they then approach these chores, they will be less likely to go through mental objections before they eventually, inevitably do the work. They just do it without thinking about it. Some advice: start young, don't expect perfection, do expect battles, stay calm, stay kind, praise and thank your children, and keep a teaching mentality. It is kindness to teach our children to do things they don't feel like doing.

Money has a prominent place in life, and how we handle it has a profound impact on the daily flow of our lives. Self-discipline in the area of finances is a character trait that will serve our children well. It is kindness to train our children in Christian principles of tithing and budgeting.

Learning to share is an important task of childhood, and

it doesn't usually happen naturally. Just observe a church toddler nursery, and you'll witness "survival of the fittest" in action. As parents, we must repeatedly instruct our children to share, and we must physically guide their behavior and nurture their emotions. When our children were young, I tried an experiment. I sat on the floor and played with two of them. Instead of waiting for an argument, I spoke in a very sweet voice and told one child to give the other a toy. I gave reasons for it such as: "He would really like that," and "You have two of those. Wouldn't it be nice if you shared one?" When the child shared, I offered profuse praise and hugs. I believe we can teach children the joy of sharing at a young age by rewarding them and letting them gain positive associations with generosity.

"He that is soon angry dealeth foolishly.... He that is slow to wrath is of great understanding: but he that is hasty of spirit exalteth folly" (Prov. 14:17a, 29). Do you want to rear a foolish child or one of great understanding? A gentle and wise mother of ten children once told me, "Between twelve and eighteen months of age, you are likely to have a major power struggle with your child, and the older they are, the harder it is to win the battle."

I distinctly remember one such battle. A distinguished theologian was having lunch at our house when one of our children, at the age of one-and-a-half years, decided that this was the time. As our child's anger began to steam out of control, I excused us and calmly departed for the privacy of the bedroom. I'm sure the walls did not muffle the enraged screaming and crying. After administering discipline, I repeatedly laid our child down in bed and said like a broken record, "You may not speak to Mommy in that way. You must obey Mommy. You must take a nap." Finally, the calm returned and, by God's grace, we have never experienced a fraction of that resistance since.

Part of controlling the emotions is breaking the will while being careful not to defeat the spirit. Negative reinforcement of negative emotions and positive reinforcement of positive emotions at a young age mold a child's inner psyche, so he or she can live without being dragged down by self-defeating impulses. How much crime is committed in a fit of anger and regretted moments later? A moment's loss of self-control reaps years in jail. It's a tragedy. In daily life, controlling our emotions leads to better relations at home and in society, and it can even bring promotions and broader opportunities. We think of strong emotions as having great power, but Proverbs 16:32 asserts that "he that is slow to anger is better than the mighty; and he that ruleth his spirit than he that taketh a city." It is a great kindness to teach our children to restrain and channel their emotions.

Be a kind police

A boy once told his mom that when he was little he thought about keeping a dollar bill that was left over from his church money. He decided against it. When she asked him why, he said, "Because I thought I would get caught." As I reflect on my own childhood and the types of misbehavior that I needed to be pulled away from, I believe it was that same influence that kept me from repeating certain sins. It is necessary for children to feel the all-pervasive eye of a parent on them when they are young. It lays the foundation for the development of the conscience. A young child thinks in terms of cause and effect. "If I do this, then this will happen." It's not until years later, in some cases many years, that he or she operates on the level of doing what is morally right.

I believe God equipped mothers with a sense that enables us to pay attention to several different things at one time. We can be cooking dinner, but we are aware of other things that are happening in the house. We partially tune out when things are calm, but we are alert when danger or naughtiness arises. It is kindness to nip naughtiness in the bud.

Love of learning

Dan and his two brothers are educators, filling positions of teacher, principal, or superintendent. I asked them what their parents did that prompted all three of them to go into education. One of them answered, "Our parents gave us many opportunities to learn, which we had no choice but to participate in." I vowed to myself at that moment I would do the same for our children. The very words *teaching* and *learning* cause excitement to well up inside of me. But it wasn't always that way. "I can't wait to get out of here!" was a frequent refrain of mine during my elementary and high school years. It took a number of years to emerge, but somehow my parents and teachers instilled in me a love for learning. We do our children a great favor if we instill in them excitement to learn about God's creation all around us. One way to nurture a thirst for knowledge is to make family vacations educational instead of purely entertaining. Another way is to instruct our children about their sur-roundings, like local history or how the water system works, during the course of daily life. We may be met with resistance, but if we persevere, the results will follow. It is kindness to teach our children to love learning.

Contentment

"Count your blessings."

"Think about the starving children in Africa."

"Life is not always fair. That's just the way things are."

Every parent has uttered these platitudes, and children roll their eyes. But they are true, and we ought not give up on teaching their principles. We must simply couch them in terms our children will hear. In a calm, instructive voice we can say:

"I'm amazed at the Lord's generosity to us. We have a nice home, plenty of food, and many other good things."

"I heard on the radio today that most children in Nigeria only eat one meal a day."

"That's too bad your team had all the bad players. Oh well, it'll be OK. I had something like that happen to me, too, today."

Part of our sinful human nature is an inclination towards selfishness. If we have a little, we tend to want more. If we have a lot, we want still more, thinking it will bring us happiness. We want things our way, at our time. We spend a lot of emotional energy dreaming of having a greater degree of happiness in the future. Studies have shown that people in rich countries are not much happier than people in poor countries. And in the United States, as long as one is not living in poverty, more money doesn't mean more happiness.[5]

Isn't it more peaceful and sensible to think realistically of the future, devise a plan for getting there, and enjoy the present? We do our best to live according to Scripture, and if God's providence hands us events we don't like, we know He is in control. Better yet, He promises to help us through. If we have a spirit of contentment, the effect will spill over to our children. Paul's words are wise: "Godliness with contentment is great gain" (1 Tim. 6:6). It is kindness to model contentment to our children.

A place for teasing

Teasing is part of life. It can run the gamut from loving words of endearment to mean-spirited cruelty. Some families tease; others don't. It seems that brothers have a penchant for teasing sisters. What is a healthy balance? We use the "pain factor" in our home. Some members of our family are more sensitive than others. Good-natured teasing, with no harm intended or received, is a way to show love and give attention while acknowledging our foibles and idiosyncrasies. There's nothing wrong with that. It can help us laugh at ourselves. But when the recipient of the teasing is hurt or irritated, the teaser ought to stop. Other members of the family can smooth the rough spots by saying, "It's OK, Lydia, Calvin didn't mean it in a bad way. It's really pretty funny, isn't it?" Kindness must be at the root of all our interactions in the home. Some families do a lot of teasing; it is an integral part of their communication. Even though some of it seems unkind to me, I can't judge them, because I am probably overly sensitive and too easily hurt. I do ask them to examine themselves and be aware of those who might be more sensitive. Is there a kinder, more loving way to carry out the teasing?

We must be concerned when teasing gets negative,

intentionally hurtful, cruel, or physically damaging. God does not look lightly on this. "Whoso mocketh the poor reproacheth his Maker: and he that is glad at calamities shall not be unpunished" (Prov. 17:5). Discipline is necessary in such cases, especially if cruel teasing is done on the sly. Discussing this behavior with our children helps them to understand themselves and the feelings of others. Is anger, revenge, hurt, inferiority, or jealousy the driving force? We need to dig deeply enough to get to the bottom of mean-spirited teasing. If we want our children to be considerate and not walk on others for their own gratification, we simply must nip unkindness in the bud.

Simple kindness

The most basic aspect of teaching kindness to our children is simply to teach them to "be ye kind, one to another" (Eph. 4:32). So much of life is made up of the little things: speaking nicely, helping a friend in need, sharing, not hitting, and so forth. Yet even the little things have the heart as their fountainhead. And in a sense, the fountainhead of the children is the parents. Our daily task is to teach our children kindness. As we monitor their behavior, we must check the pulse of their heart of kindness. When José pinches his brother, is it innocent horseplay or is it a desire to inflict pain? When Heather sobs over losing a prize, is she just tired or is selfishness creeping in?

We love our children with everything that is in us. Let's pray that God gives us the wisdom to model and instruct them in the way of kindheartedness. Let's pray for perseverance. Let's pray God they arrive at that honorable goal.

"Be ye kind, one to another" (Eph. 4:32).

1. James Dobson, *The New Strong-Willed Child* (Wheaton, Ill.: Tyndale House Publishers, Inc., 2004), 38–41.

2. Robert Karen, *Becoming Attached* (Oxford: Oxford University Press, 1994), 17.

3. James Dobson, *The New Strong-Willed Child* (Wheaton, Ill.: Tyndale House Publishers, Inc., 2004), 119–132.

4. For practical guidance in these areas, see Joel Beeke's *Bringing the Gospel to Covenant Children* (Grand Rapids: Reformation Heritage Books, 2002) and *Family Worship* (Grand Rapids: Reformation Heritage Books, 2004).

5. Alison Grant. "Rich get richer, but not happier," *Grand Rapids Press*, February 6, 2005, H4.

CHAPTER 7
The Teacher's Role

Parents hold the most important key to unlocking kindness in the heart of a child. Teachers are next in line. The foundation is laid at home during the first, critical years of learning, but the pathway a child takes in the area of kindness can vary greatly during the school years.

Picture a relay race. The child is the baton. Dad and Mom (it's best if both are involved) carry the child through the preschool years. With each passing grade, the parents and the individual teachers carry the child together. At the end of the race of childhood, we launch the child onto the sea of independence, hoping and praying the training we have given him will successfully carry him through adulthood.

Teachers must focus on academics. That is their job. Math, reading, science, and such subjects are very important. But the teacher who conveys only the subject matter misses incredible opportunities to mold the life of a child in ways that will affect him lifelong. First Corinthians 13:2 states that even if I can prophesy, understand all mysteries, understand all knowledge, and have enough faith to move a mountain, but don't possess charity or love, I am nothing.

Teaching is exhausting work. I know; I have been there. But I challenge every teacher consciously to weave into the fabric of your daily lessons the instruction of kindness. Students who only gain knowledge and information and then fail to internalize values such as honesty, diligence, generosity, loyalty, patience, self-control, courage, and compassion are like a machine with no lubrication. The parts are all there, but the machine won't run smoothly without the oil that reduces the friction of everyday life. I would like to suggest some practical ways to carry out the instruction of kindness in the school setting.

Everything that applies to parents (Chapter 6) applies to teachers as well. Based on that foundation, teachers can continue instruction about kindness in the classroom. Those early years are foundational; a diamond in the rough is very valuable, but it needs to be cut and polished for it to shine in its full glory. Some kindergarten diamonds are rougher than others. But every child, every eternal soul, is a God-created diamond. Age-appropriate instruction at every level of education is essential.

Unfortunately, we don't live in a perfect world. Some students have to unlearn negative behavior before teachers can make progress with positive instruction. And then there is the characteristic of original sin that we all bear, which is painfully evident in every classroom on earth. But the general rule is that persistence, with God's blessing, will win in the end. "Train up a child in the way he should go: and when he is old, he will not depart from it" (Prov. 22:6). We cannot expect immediate results. Principles learned in childhood are often submerged until the adult years when they surface. Each of us has to look no further than the mirror to acknowledge this fact. Perseverance, with an eye on long-term goals, is necessary.

Interwoven

When weaving fabric, the foundational threads that stretch lengthwise on the loom are called the "warp threads." The "weft threads" are woven crosswise in various patterns and colors. The weft threads draw our attention, but things would fall apart without the drab-colored warp threads. Likewise, in education, the curriculum of language arts, math, the sciences, and the arts are the weft threads, but things would fall apart if values such as honesty, diligence, loyalty, and perseverance were not taught. Kindness is one of those warp threads that must be woven into education.

Examine your own philosophy. Do you value kindness? At the very minimum, your own example, your manner of teaching, and the flavor of your words must show kindness. Teachers do care about children. Even when your patience wears thin and the paperwork is mountainous, get back in touch with those convictions and feelings that may have grown cold. Prayer is the best way to accomplish this because God cares greatly for all His creatures, and He alone can bring our hearts in line with His.

Here are some practical ways of interweaving kindness into your teaching without ever making an extra lesson plan:

1. *Don't play favorites.* Ever. Kids have very perceptive radars for fairness, and they will detect unfairness before you are even aware you are showing it.

2. *Pay attention to who is left out.* Notice who is alone when groups are picked. Pick the groups yourself if there is a possibility someone will be left out. Who is standing alone in the hallway? Place him with an outgoing person in work groups. A smile and a kind word from a teacher can

bring cheer to a dreary day. Be kind to the underdog, but be careful not to show favoritism to him. Every child is talented in some way; find a way to recognize and appreciate that value.

3. *Keep your ears and eyes open for teasing or bullying at recess or break times.* Those who practice these behaviors are often masters of stealth, but sometimes it leaks out. Address it immediately, aggressively, firmly, but with kindness.

4. *Monitor your tone of voice.* Keep it calm, kind, and firm. Only yell if there is a fire. Never be sarcastic. Be pleasant. Force it, if you must! Smile with your whole face. Give compliments. Say nice things.

5. *Be tuned in to what is going on in the personal lives of your students.* Sometimes negative behavior is an outgrowth of something else happening in their lives. Is marital discord or divorce of parents affecting the child? Is a student depressed? Is a child being abused? Yes, it could be the tip of an iceberg you would rather not discover, but you could be instrumental in averting a Titanic disaster. Delegate the issue to a professional if it is too big for you to handle.

6. *Is a student developing habits of lying or stealing?* Is he defiant or lazy? Has he had pornography in his posses- sion or spoken about it? It is kindness to discipline such dangerous behavior when it has just begun. If ignored, these traits grow insidiously and may eventually damage or destroy a person.

7. *Discipline and kindness are not mutually exclusive.* In fact, they go hand-in-hand. It is a kindness to discipline. But do discipline with dignity. Even bullies need to be treated with dignity. Each soul is created by God. Where there is

life, there is hope. A teacher's attitude of high expectations can motivate a student to a higher plateau of behavior.

8. *Exercise empathy.* Some are tough, some are soft, but all children care about themselves. They have tender feelings, and teachers do well to get inside the emotions and motives that make each child tick. Students can sense if you care about them, even in discipline.

9. *Be careful how you speak about others to the students.* Use stories to show respect to people from all walks of life. Stories of negative examples are necessary for children to learn lessons from the mistakes of others, but they can still be presented in a kind way.

10. *Pray.* Who is able to do all that a teacher ought to do? Jesus said, "My grace is sufficient for thee: for my strength is made perfect in weakness" (2 Cor. 12:9).

Teachers hold an inestimable position in society. Did you know that the average student in America spends 14,040 hours in school during his elementary and secondary education? If teachers can flavor their teaching with kindness and instill this character trait in their students, they will leave an amazing and valuable legacy.

Going beyond

Some teachers are able to go beyond weaving kindness into their daily lessons when their schools include values education in the curriculum, of which kindness is one component.

There are a variety of approaches. An entire school can focus on one value per month by means of assemblies, bulletin boards, classroom activities incorporated into various subject areas, and rewards for positive behavior.

There are literature-based programs that teach morals through stories, accompanied by reflective writing and discussions. Instruction can range from a few minutes of devotions focused on a moral to actively serving in the community. The goal of each program is to instill values into the child not only during the course of the instruction, but for a lifetime. It is good when a child carries on a habit such as kindness because he has learned it well, but it is wonderful when a child internalizes kindness because he has experienced the worth and the joy of it. This virtue will then shine brighter and longer.

I have sketched basic ways kindness can be promoted in the school setting. If only this positive teaching were enough to insure kindness between students! Unfortunately, the reality of our sinful nature jolts us awake. Unkindness happens, and it happens a lot at school. Teachers must be prepared to deal with the negative behavior of students. The next chapter focuses on bullying, which can appear in many forms—some mild, some cruel.

CHAPTER 8
Bullying

⁓•••⁓

His neck seemed crooked at birth, and there was a lump that grew quickly. It was diagnosed as cystic hygroma and surgically removed. But the problem resurfaced as an infection in his tongue, causing him to ooze and drool blackish red secretions. His tongue was scabbed and swollen and he could hardly eat, so he didn't grow much. Surgery carved out part of his tongue, but the problem remained. Stares and "Oh, yuck!" greeted him from children and even some adults. But his family showered him with love and care, so he thrived. Then he began school. Kindergarten started off okay, but, as the awe of school wore off, the teasing began about his scab-covered tongue that hung out. He didn't want to go back for first grade and kept running home. The teasing was incessant. His parents complained to the teachers and principal, but he later acknowledged that "no amount of adult supervision could prevent the arrows from piercing my heart on the playground, in physical education class, or in the school bathrooms, away from the watchful eyes of the teachers."[1]

It continued in high school—the shoving, throwing, hitting, and mocking. His way of coping was to create monsters: in his imagination, in stories, and in structures he would build. He was taught not to fight back, though he wished he could. He was taught that God had a purpose in his life. It took decades, but he became a successful author of Christian fiction.

Then Eric Harris and Dylan Klebold carried out their Columbine High School massacre. This man heard about the circumstances of their lives, including the harassment they received from fellow students. He felt God urging him to reveal his own story of suffering. The subdued response of 5,500 people at a Life on the Edge seminar made him think he flopped. But one by one, people came up to him, telling their own stories of teasing and abuse, and he knew he had opened some wounds. His name is Frank Peretti, and he has since written *No More Bullies*, an autobiographical book on how to deal with bullying.[2] It is a book every teacher, parent, bus driver, or anyone who works with children and teens *must* read.

We tend to think of bullying as boys' behavior, but this is not so. Rachel Simmons, in *Odd Girl Out*, draws our attention to the tactics of aggression that some girls use. "There is a hidden culture of girls' aggression in which bullying is epidemic, distinctive, and destructive. It is not marked by the direct physical and verbal behavior that is primarily the province of boys. Girls use backbiting, exclusion, rumors, name-calling, and manipulation to inflict psychological pain on targeted victims. Unlike boys, who tend to bully acquaintances or strangers, girls frequently attack within tightly knit networks of friends, making aggression harder to identify and intensifying the damage to the victims. Within the hidden culture of aggression, girls fight with body language and relationships instead of fists and knives."[3]

Special attention needs to be directed at bullying. Bullying is unkindness taken to an extreme. It goes beyond good-natured ribbing. If left unattended, it can cause lifelong emotional scars on the victim and scars of a different sort on the bully—scars and habits that will be harder to break the longer they are perpetuated. One of four bullies ends up having brushes with the law.[4] Teachers, even more than parents, are on the front lines of the part of this battle that often takes place at school. Bullying has spread in recent years, and has crept into the privacy of our homes by way of cyberbullying. Parents need to be equipped to fight this cruelty.

Bullying defined

What is bullying? We must not define it too broadly and become overprotective of our children to the point that they are not prepared to deal with the bumps of life, nor must we define it too narrowly and ignore the potential harm our children might be exposed to.

A mother and daughter team, Suellen Fried and Paula Fried, in their book *Bullies and Victims*, distinguish harmful and non-harmful teasing. They describe six factors that are present in harmful teasing.

1. *Intent to harm:* the perpetrator finds pleasure in the taunting and continues even when the victim's distress is obvious.
2. *Intensity and duration:* the teasing continues over a long period of time and the degree of taunting is damaging to the self-esteem of the victim.

3. *Power of the abuser:* the abuser maintains power because of age, strength, size, and/or gender.
4. *Vulnerability of the victim:* the victim is more sensitive to teasing, cannot adequately defend him or herself, and has physical or psychological qualities that make him or her more prone to vulnerability.
5. *Lack of support:* the victim feels isolated and exposed. Often, the victim is afraid to report the abuse for fear of retaliation.
6. *Consequence:* the damage to self-concept is long lasting, and the impact on the victim leads to behavior marked by either withdrawal or aggression.[5]

Next, we must identify the various types of bullying. The Frieds describe four categories: physical, verbal, emotional, and sexual abuse.

Physical abuse can include "punching, poking, strangling, suffocating, bending fingers back, burning, poisoning, hair pulling, excessive tickling, biting, stabbing, and shooting."[6] Since the early 1970s, school violence has increased dramatically,[7] although school crime has been gradually decreasing after peaking in 1993.[8] There were 2.7 million school crimes reported in 1998. Of these, 9% were serious violent crimes like murder, rape, sexual assault, robbery, and aggravated assault; while 33% were simple assault and 58% were theft.[9] There were twenty-two school-related deaths in 2000–2001.[10] It is unacceptable that 160,000 children miss school every day because they are afraid of attack or intimidation.[11]

Verbal abuse is "the use of words as cruelty to a child's physical, moral, or mental well-being."[12] It is recognized by any of the six criteria above, and it can escalate into sexual abuse. This is the most common form of bullying and likely the most under-reported. It can be carried out as simply as a whispered "you're ugly" in passing. Cyberbullying happens when the bully sends abusive messages electronically. Verbal abuse can appear in the form of teasing, mocking, humiliation, gossip, character assassination, yelling, and threatening. It can be launched for many reasons: good or bad grades, handicaps, beauty or lack thereof, speech patterns, hair color, glasses, braces, body shape, any physical characteristic that is out of the ordinary, or simply for being new at school. Motives for verbal abuse may be jealousy, anger, unkindness, pride, inferiority, revenge, or lack of forethought or empathy. In Chapter 11, the incredible power of words is dealt with in more depth.

Emotional abuse can include rejecting, terrorizing, isolating, and corrupting.[13] Coupled with verbal abuse, it is the weapon of choice for girls more than for boys. It is harder to define and detect because it is less tangible than the other types of abuse, but its consequences can be equally or more devastating. It can occur in isolation or with other forms of abuse, but the result is the diminished value of another so that the victim believes himself to be unworthy of respect, friendship, love, or protection.[14] Emotional abuse can be actively carried out with words, actions, and nonverbal behavior, or it can be passively carried out by withholding positive behavior. Rejection is common; for example, a classmate might be excluded because she doesn't dress nicely or is overweight. All of us experience rejection upon occasion, but if it is done cruelly or consistently, these experiences can have lifelong effects. An extreme example is the failure-to-thrive child who does not receive the nurture he needs at home and does not eat, exercise, or grow normally. Terrorizing is more intentional. It involves threatening another person, resulting in fear of humiliation or harm. Isolating deprives children of normal social interaction. It is not uncommon for girls to campaign among peers to leave one girl out. It is intentionally designed to hurt. Corruption happens when a child is encouraged to engage in negative behavior such as substance abuse, or physical or sexual aggression.

Sexual abuse between peers occurs when sexual inter-actions are coercive, exploitive, or aggressive, or when they threaten the physical or psychological well-being of either participant.[15] There is a wide range. Non-contact abuse includes exhibitionism, voyeurism, verbal sexual propositions, or harassment. Contact sexual abuse includes penetration and non-penetration sexual activity. Because the sexual aspect of our being is so profoundly personal, the deepest of scars can result from certain types of sexual abuse.

Abuse in school is not a pretty picture. No battlefield is. Even after the bullies and victims exit and all is quiet, the scars cry out for healing. Maybe you have some; it is quite likely that someone near you does. This is a battle that must be fought. It won't ever be completely won; it is continuous. But there is much hope; there are many ways to rein in bullying. In Edmund Burke's words, "The only thing necessary for the triumph of evil is for good men to do nothing."[16]

No choice

Let no teacher underestimate the importance of entering this fray. If you are a teacher, it is essential that you be tuned in to bullying and that you attack it with all the power and wisdom you can muster. No teacher should say, "We don't ever have that problem here." You teach sinners; some sinners bully.

You can't say, "That is what boys and girls do; it's part of life," and simply ignore it. It's true; it is what children do, but it is also sin. We address sins like stealing and cheating, but do we allow the bullies to do their destructive work behind the scenes?

Some people feel it is good for children to "toughen each other up." There is a degree to which children must learn to fight their own battles, but bullying goes beyond this. The bully needs to be accountable to the command to love God above all and his neighbor as himself, and the victim needs instruction in preventing or handling the abuse, and in some cases protection and assistance from peers or adults.

Maybe you are unsure of how to handle it. Maybe you are so overwhelmed just dealing with the visible problems you encounter on a normal day at school that you don't have time or energy to deal with the under-the-radar problems. Take heart. God's Word gives guidance and much new study has been made on the subject of bullying. Being equipped with the tools will enable you to make headway in the battle against bullying.

God's perspective

How do we deal with this challenging problem? We certainly need the wisdom of Solomon. To give a perspective on what God thinks of cruelty, Solomon tells us seven things God hates: "A proud look, a lying tongue, and hands that shed innocent blood, an heart that deviseth wicked imaginations, feet that be swift in running to mischief, a false witness that speaketh lies, and he that soweth discord among brethren" (Prov. 6:17–19). Isn't it amazing that of all the sins in the world, the ones that are singled out here all appear in some form in bullying? If God takes these sins so seriously, so ought we.

God also promises He will intervene. This is a great consolation to the victim of bullying. "Whoso diggeth a pit shall fall therein: and he that rolleth a stone, it will return upon him" (Prov. 26:27). Scripture is replete with this theme. God will deal with wickedness. In modern language, "What goes around, comes around." Those who practice cruelty will receive cruelty. Those who are kind will receive kindness.

God often uses difficulties in our lives to draw us close to Him, console us, admonish us, or instruct us. This is an important part of the Christian life and of God's plan. You may wonder why God allows such bad things to happen. If a person is bullied, cries out to God for help, is born again in the process, and is saved from going to hell, isn't it worth it? Adults in authority are responsible to fight bullying with all their might, but God can still use it for good.

God offers hope and rescue to those who are persecuted. He cares for the creatures of His creation. His tender lovingkindness shines through. He urges the victim, "Call upon me in the day of trouble: I will deliver thee, and thou shalt glorify me" (Ps. 50:15). For those who suffer for the honor Christ, one of the beatitudes reads, "Blessed are ye, when men shall revile you, and persecute you, and shall say all manner of evil against you falsely, for my sake. Rejoice, and be exceeding glad: for great is your reward in heaven;

for so persecuted they the prophets which were before you: (Matt. 5:11–12).

The victim of bullying can find consolation from biblical characters. Joseph was ostracized, sold as a slave, maligned, and forgotten in spite of diligently doing what was right. David's life was threatened and his kingship was almost stolen, even though he was a man after God's own heart. Jeremiah was vilified and thrown into a slime pit for prophesying God's words. Paul was beaten, imprisoned, stoned, and hounded for preaching the gospel.

Most of all, Jesus was "bullied" to the greatest degree possible. At age thirty-three, He lived out His teachings. He stood alone before powerful men and endured false accusations. The crowds shouted, "Crucify Him!" His friends deserted Him for fear of their own lives. The soldiers whipped His back with bone-studded strips of leather and imbedded a crown of thorns into His head. The mobs ridiculed Him by dressing Him as the king that He was—although they didn't believe that He was king. They challenged His omnipotence by goading Him to save Himself from the excruciating pain of hanging on the cross. Jesus gave His life to His persecutors. He understands like no one else can. And He is immediately available through prayer to the one who is bullied.

Our action

What ought our action to be, based on God's advice? Our natural inclination is to turn the Golden Rule around. "Do unto him as he has just done to me." We want the bully to suffer the same pain he is inflicting on us. It seems logical, but it often doesn't work, according to authorities on bullying.

And it is not the Lord's way. "Recompense to no man evil for evil.... Dearly beloved, avenge not yourselves, but rather give place unto wrath: for it is written, Vengeance is mine; I will repay, saith the Lord" (Rom. 12:17a, 19). Does this mean we simply do nothing in response to cruelty? Certainly not. It means our driving motivation in dealing with bullying is not anger or retaliation, but remediation and healing. What about self-defense? Scripture doesn't prevent us from protecting ourselves, but our motive must not be revenge. "But there must be something we can do," you might say.

There is. We have to go beyond "no evil for evil" to overcoming evil with good (Rom. 12:21). Jesus teaches us in Luke 6:27–29, "But I say unto you which hear, Love your enemies, do good to them which hate you, bless them that curse you, and pray for them which despitefully use you. And unto him that smiteth thee on the one cheek offer also the other; and him that taketh away thy cloak forbid not to take thy coat also." Solomon's wisdom is, "If thine enemy be hungry, give him bread to eat; and if he be thirsty, give him water to drink: for thou shalt heap coals of fire upon his head, and the LORD shall reward thee" (Prov. 25:21–22). The reasons for doing so are threefold. First, God tells us to. Second, the meaning behind heaping coals of fire upon his head is to show kindness to our enemies so that they will repent and change. It means if their fire goes out, we share our coals with them. The third reason is that the Lord will reward us.

The principle of returning good for evil, rather than evil for evil, doesn't seem to make sense. It is not founded on logic; it is founded on grace. Jesus' instruction was not empty rhetoric. He of all people could have annihilated each one of His persecutors and walked away unscathed. But He didn't because He had a higher goal than His own immediate deliverance. He was working for the eternal deliverance of His adopted sons and daughters—for those who sin against Him, yet are drawn to Him with sorrow for their sins and with faith in Him. By paying the full price for our sins, He set an example that lasts into eternity. If we have received His grace and mercy, we will strive to show grace and mercy to others, even to our bullies.

Contemporary wisdom

Since the early 1990s, the subject of bullying has undergone unprecedented study. Scholars in the fields of education and psychology have dragged the bullies out of the shady alcoves of our schools and neighborhoods and exposed their cruelty to the light of day. Their studies offer valuable explanations and solutions for this problem.

Where does bullying come from? The short answer is sinful hearts. A more detailed answer includes jealousy, anger, unresolved needs, insecurity, selfishness, lack of empathy, deprivation of love, deprivation of parental control, abuse, lack of self-control, immaturity, lack of knowledge of conflict resolution, a controlling personality, misunderstanding, misjudging motives, retaliation, impatience, exposure to violence, or desire for violence. Bullying doesn't usually appear out of the blue. Teachers and parents can be more effective and empathetic if we understand the backgrounds of our children.

There is one source that warrants our special attention. It is the violence to which our children and teens are exposed in music, on TV, in movies, and in video games.

How can witnessing eight thousand murders and a hundred thousand acts of violence (73% of them unpunished) by the end of grade school *not* numb our children to real-life violence?[17] A remote village in Canada did not have television access until 1973. Social scientists monitored the rate of inappropriate physical aggression among forty-five first and second graders and found that, after two years of television exposure, the rate increased 160 percent in both boys and girls.[18] Many other studies bear this out. Police records of many cities cite crimes that were copied from TV. Hollywood doesn't seem to care beyond the dollar signs. It is up to parents, educators, and anyone who cares about children to rise up and fight the forces that are destroying our youth.

So what do we do? There are certain ingredients that successful anti-bullying programs have in common. They are summarized in the following list.

1. Knowledge about the nature of bullying is vital. How can we fight the enemy if we don't recognize and understand him? Seminars for teachers are a wonderful way to inform and inspire educators to battle bullying. A school-wide program allows teachers to stand shoulder to shoulder, decreasing the chances of the bully slipping through undetected.

2. Everyone must get involved. Bullies need to learn not to bully. Victims need to learn how to prevent or deal with bullying. Witnesses have an obligation to deter the bully and assist the victim. Teachers and administrators must instruct, motivate, supervise, and model. Because the home is still the most influential force on a child's behavior, no successful anti-bullying pro-

gram is complete without instruction to the parents, especially with the emergence of cyberbullying.

3. The younger the children are taught, the more successful the program is. Preschool is not too young. We don't have to wait for bullying to reach our radar screen. It is quite possibly happening behind the scenes. Children who know about bullies and victims are more prepared to deal with both presently or in the future. Young children are far more likely to discuss experiences and observations openly. And if a bully's deeds are uncovered, he or she is more moldable. Also, a younger victim will seek help. The situation in junior and senior high is vastly different; the bully has become more sophisticated in his methods, including threatening his victims. The victim is paralyzed by the fear of being a tattler and would rather endure the bullying than risk the consequences of retaliation.

4. Be aware of the general differences between the bullying techniques of boys and girls. Boys are usually more direct, using physical and verbal abuse against acquaintances or strangers. Girls are often more covert, directing verbal, nonverbal, and emotional abuse at their friends.[19]

5. Modify the environment. Arrange seating to minimize conflict. Pick teams by numbering off "1-2-1-2" rather than leaving an unathletic student to be picked last every time. Ask parents to monitor the playground.

6. Communicate clear expectations to students and back them up with consequences. Children know whether unkindness is unacceptable or ignored.

7. Don't encourage kids to fight back. It doesn't solve the problem; rather, it escalates it.

8. It is easy to become focused on the negative nature of bullying, but positive alternatives are a big part of the solution. Here are some ideas:

    a. Some innovative teachers assigned junior high students to present an anti-bullying lesson to lower-elementary students and found it resulted in less bullying by both groups.

    b. Providing constructive outlets for anger and frustration can decrease hurtful behavior. Physical exercise helps divert negative energy in a positive direction. Just listening to a child's concerns can help defuse a volatile situation. It is far better for a child to join a club or team with activities that reflect his skills than for him to join a gang. Teens crave belonging to a group.

    c. Searching for the bully's motives can help us understand his behavior and offer solutions. The playground bully might be abused at home.

    d. The goal of empathy training is to cause bullies to internalize the Golden Rule. Each person is uniquely created and ought to be valued.

    e. Serving others can open up a whole new world to young people. They learn to focus on the needs of others and think less selfishly.

    f. Conflict resolution has been highly successful in bringing creative solutions to difficult situations, especially when peers are involved with adults.

    g. By placing anti-bullying measures in the framework of lifelong goals, we can motivate students to think

and behave in ways that will reap immediate and long-term benefits.
h. Try kindness. We all desire comfort, care, and kindness—even bullies do. We have to deal with the bad behavior while utilizing opportunities to show love and affirmation.

It is a battle—a battle between good and evil. But there is much cause for hope and optimism. Let's be encouraged, roll up our sleeves, and get to work. If we do nothing, evil will prosper. Let's pray for strength and wisdom, and then set about the task of fighting bullying with the tools God has given us.

1. Frank Peretti, *The Wounded Spirit* (later entitled *No More Bullies*) (Nashville, Tenn.: Word Publishing, 2000), 50.

2. Ibid.

3. Rachel Simmons, *Odd Girl Out* (San Diego: Harcourt, Inc., 2002), 3.

4. Suellen Fried and Paula Fried, *Bullies and Victims* (New York: M. Evans and Company, 1996), 49.

5. Ibid., 9–10.

6. Ibid., 13.

7. Ibid., 17.

8. School Violence Resource Center, "Fact Sheet: School Crime Statistics," University of Arkansas System, Criminal Justice Institute (Little Rock, Ark.), August 2001, http://www.svrc.net/Files/ProbabilityFactSheet.pdf (accessed August 3, 2007).

9. Ibid.

10. Ibid.

11. Fried, 20.

12. Fried, 32.

13. Fried, 45.

14. Fried, 45.

15. Fried, 55.

16. Edmund Burke to William Smith, January 9, 1795, in *Bartlett's Familiar Quotations*, ed. Emily Morison Beck (Boston: Little, Brown, 1968), 454.

17. Fried, 27, 178.

18. Fried, 178.

19. Simmons, 3.

CHAPTER 9

A Letter to Children and Teens

⸺⸻◦•◦⸻⸺

Dear children and teens,

Who are you, and what kind of person are you? How do you relate to others in your class, to those who are younger or older, and to your brothers and sisters? What is your attitude? Are you kind to others or do you bully them? Are you helpful or do you use people for your own benefit? Are you nice to those who have wronged you or do you get back at others? Maybe you fall somewhere in between the categories in these descriptions. Have you ever received kindness from someone to whom you were mean? How do you deal with your happy feelings? How do you deal with your sadness and anger?

How do others treat you? Are they kind to you? Do they give you positive attention? Do they respect you? Or do they ignore you, tease you, bully you?

Each one of you has a different personality and a different set of experiences. Like each leaf on a tree, you are unique. You are special. We each have things we like about ourselves, as well as things we wish were different. The same is true about our situations in life.

There are some things we all have in common. We want to be happy. We like others to treat us with respect and kindness. We want our needs to be met. We don't want to be unhappy, and it hurts when others treat us unkindly.

You've heard of the Golden Rule: "Do unto others as you would have them do unto you." If you are following this rule in your life, great! You are receiving joy and benefits for doing so. If you are not following this rule, I challenge you to try. I want to convince you that it is worthwhile and that you will find a kind of happiness you didn't realize you could have.

But first, here is a story. The tone is at a child's level, but the content is good for any age. It is entitled "Robert's Revenge."[1]

Robert listened as his teacher read their memory text for the week. "'Therefore if thine enemy hunger, feed him; if he thirst, give him drink: for in so doing thou shalt heap coals of fire on his head.' This text can be found in Romans 12:20. Can anyone tell me what this means?"

Before anyone could raise a hand to answer, Robert clenched his fists and hissed, "No!"

"Excuse me, Robert," Mrs. Burns said, "Don't you understand the text?"

"Yes, I understand," he answered hotly, "but I will never do that!"

"See me after class, Robert. Perhaps then you can explain why you feel as you do."

Robert sat sullenly through the rest of the lesson. After class, he waited for Mrs. Burns. When everyone else had left, Mrs. Burns called Robert to her desk and said, "Now Robert, please explain why you behaved as you did during our Bible lesson."

"It's just not fair!" Robert burst out. "If you had an

enemy like I have, you wouldn't be nice to him either. You would rather see him starve!"

"Why, Robert!" Mrs. Burns exclaimed. "How can you say such a thing? Whatever happened to make you feel so bitter?"

Anger burned in Robert's throat as he told Mrs. Burns his story. "Peter lives in the same apartment building as I do. He is always doing mean things to me. Yesterday just as I was coming home from school, he called to me from a window on the fourth floor. He had Jessie, my favorite cat, and threatened to throw her down. I screamed, 'No! Please don't hurt Jessie!' But he just laughed and threw her down anyway." Here Robert's voice broke with a sob and Mrs. Burns put her arm around his shaking shoulder.

"Did Jessie get hurt?" she asked.

"Oh, Mrs. Burns," he said through his tears, "I picked her up and placed her in my own bed. I slept on the floor and kept checking her all night. But this morning, Jessie was dead! I had to find a place where I could bury her before school this morning."

"Oh, Robert!" Mrs. Burns tried to comfort him. "Peter did a very wicked thing, but our text for this week says that——"

"Never!" Robert interrupted. "Never would I help him! And even if I have to wait until I am a man, I will get even with him!" Before Mrs. Burns could try to reason with him, Robert ran from the room.

Robert ran outside, only to find that it was raining and a cold wind was blowing. He decided to go home, even though no one would be home from work yet. He entered the apartment and passed the door where Peter and his father lived. Peter was home alone and his door was partly open. As Robert went by, Peter mockingly said, "Meeooow! Meeoow!"

Robert turned pale with anger. He put his hands over his ears and ran up to his apartment. He went to his own room, threw himself across his bed, and muttered, "And we are supposed to give food to somebody like that if they are hungry? Never!" Robert fell asleep that night filled with thoughts of hatred for Peter.

The next morning as Robert hurried past Peter's door on his way to school, he heard someone crying. He stopped and cautiously approached the door. It was partly open so he looked into the room. There lay Peter on his bed with flushed cheeks, burning with fever. "Oh Robert," he groaned when he saw him standing in the doorway, "please call the landlady. My dad is gone and I feel so terrible. I need help!"

"Really? You feel terrible? Well, good! I'm glad to hear it!" Robert made an ugly face at Peter and left, closing Peter's door firmly so no one would hear him cry for help. Robert hurried off to school, whistling happily. He hoped that Peter would be sick for a long time.

Robert was happier than usual all day. It didn't even bother him that he had to deliver his papers in the rain after school. He hurried through his route so he could get home, hoping Peter was still sick. But going past Peter's door, Robert saw that a light was on and Mrs. Clark, the landlady, was with him. "Now Peter, just drink this and then maybe you can sleep for awhile," she was saying. "I need to go back to work, or dinner will never be ready on time."

Robert was sorry to see that Peter was being helped. Waiting until Mrs. Clark returned to the kitchen, he went to Peter's room. Leaning against the doorframe, Robert asked, "Well, how are things going? Are you enjoying yourself now?" Robert was trying to sound mean, but Peter was too sick to notice. "Oh, Robert!" he groaned. "I am so full of pain, I have such a bad headache. My head is burning like coals of fire." Hearing the words "coals of fire," Robert turned pale. Fresh anger swept through him as he remembered the words of the text. Without saying another word, Robert ran back to his own room.

That night, Robert went to bed as usual, but he could not sleep. In his mind he clearly pictured the words of the text over and over again: "Coals of fire, coals of fire, coals of fire." Everywhere he looked he seemed to see these words before his eyes. He could hear the hours passing; the clock in the church tower struck one o'clock. Finally, he spoke aloud, "OK, I will do it! I will do it!" He felt as though he were speaking to an invisible enemy.

Robert fell asleep immediately, but the next morning he remembered his promise. When he came to Peter's door, however, he saw that Peter's father was with him. "Good. Then I don't have to stop," he thought. With this excuse, Robert continued on his way to school. But everything seemed to go wrong that day. He could not keep his mind on his work. Robert hurried straight home to his room after school. Still thinking about the promise he had made, he finally decided he would keep it. He did not want to lie awake again tonight.

Peter's door was partly open when Robert went down. Peter was lying with his face to the wall. Robert went up to the bed and asked in a sharp tone, "Hey, Peter, do you need anything?" How he hated even speaking to Peter! But he was determined to keep his promise.

"I am so thirsty. They forgot to bring me some water." Peter's voice sounded very weak.

"Give him drink!" muttered Robert as he got a glass of water. Then he grudgingly asked, "Are you hungry?"

Peter's answer was a terrible groan. Now Robert was faced with a problem. How could he keep the second part of the text? Leaving the room, he quickly walked to a nearby fruit market and asked to speak to the owner. "Sir, do you have any jobs that I could do for you?" he asked.

"Well, let me see. Yes, there's a fruit basket that needs to be delivered to this address."

"Thank you, sir." Robert took the basket and soon returned from delivering it. He did not get paid very much, but he used the money to buy a large, juicy orange. Returning to the apartment to Peter's room, Robert broke the orange into small pieces and helped Peter sit up to eat it. Peter's thankful expression made Robert uncomfortable. But he soon reminded him-self that he was only feeding Peter because he had to. When Peter finished the orange, Robert jumped up to leave saying, "There! I fed you and gave you something to drink. Now I have done my duty!"

As Robert started to leave, Peter called out, "Please don't go yet. It's very lonely with nobody here."

"No way! That's not included in the text," Robert said and calmly left for the night, leaving a puzzled Peter behind. But Robert continued to do small jobs at the fruit market. For several nights, he brought food and drink to Peter, but only because he felt he had to.

Then one evening, when Robert came as usual, Peter suddenly asked, "Robert, do you think I will ever get better?"

"I don't know. What makes you ask such a question?"

"Dad asked the doctor to come, but after examining me, he just shook his head. I think I am going to die. Oh, Robert! I'm so afraid! And before I die, I want to tell you I'm sorry for what I did to your cat." Peter began to sob and the ice around Robert's heart melted.

"Aw, Peter, that's okay. Jessie was pretty old and probably would have died soon anyway. Don't think about it anymore. But I hope you are not going to die! I will help take care of you as much as I can, Peter!"

That night Robert knelt beside his bed. He saw that the text was right. He must not try to get revenge. Now he could pray for Peter to recover. "Oh Lord," he prayed, "please help me always to do what the text says—but help me to do it from my heart. Please make Peter well again, and give us both a new heart."

How thankful Robert was to see that the Lord heard and answered his prayer! Three weeks later, he was supporting a weak Peter as they went for a walk on a warm spring day. The boys soon felt as close as brothers. They began to sit in the sun, taking turns reading from the Bible. Both boys learned to search and value God's Word. They prayed that God would teach them always to obey His will.

Can you relate to any part of this story? Are you like Peter? Or Robert? Here are some things to think about.

If you are like Robert

Maybe you are teased. Maybe someone beats you up at

school. Maybe you're simply left out. You probably feel all alone, but you're not; there are many kids like you. "That helps," you say, "but I still have to deal with it." Right, but there may be a few ways you can improve your situation.

First, try to understand what's going on. If there is any way to avoid the bullying situation, do so. I'm sure you have tried this, but take a different route. Don't go to hidden areas of the playground. Have someone with you during potential bullying situations, if possible.

In Chapter 8, I told the story of Mr. Frank Peretti. He has been where you are. He had a disease that caused an oozing tumor to protrude from his tongue. The tumor was finally taken care of, but he was small for his age because his body was busy fighting the disease. He was bullied without mercy during his school years, especially in gym class. He wrote a book about it that you should read; it is called *No More Victims*. He says, "You don't have to put up with it." He advises, "No one said that to me so I had to speak up for myself. You can, too. Stand up. Speak up. You don't have to tolerate the abuse any longer. But you may have to take the first step, at least you must be ready to respond when you see an opportunity to bring the abuse to the attention of the proper authorities."[2]

Second, try to understand your bully. What is he like and what motivates him? Maybe he's not very intelligent and feels he needs to boost himself up by being tough. Maybe she doesn't feel pretty so she cuts down others to make herself feel better. Maybe he's abused at home and only knows how to act aggressively. Regardless, your bully is not happy inside; try to understand him.

Third, realize that if your bully sees you as a person,

rather than someone on whom to take out his agressions, he is less likely to pick on you. If possible, try to talk to him— alone or with a mutual friend, away from his peers—and ask him why he bullies you, if you ever did anything wrong to him, and if it makes him happy to bully you.[3] Apologize if you have done anything wrong to him. Tell him how you feel when he bullies you. You might try to establish a bond with him; for example, if he needs some supplies for an experiment and you have them, loan them to him. Some kids have been successful in joking along with the bully. Ignoring him, rather than getting upset, might work.

Next, try to understand yourself. What is causing you to be treated like this? It is *not* your fault that you are picked on; nobody deserves this treatment. Often the apparent reason for being bullied is something you can't help. Maybe it is your size, your appearance, or your academic ability. Bullies tease for any reason. Remember, God made you as you are; you are a wonderful creation with special characteristics. For some strange reason, bullies often pick on kids that lack confidence. With help from God, your parents, your teachers, and your friends, look at yourself as that special creation. Admit your sins; then go forward, trusting in the God who made you with all your unique qualities. Let your confidence be in Him and in His gifts to you.

Then, think about this. Is it possible that there are some things you could change in order to improve your situation? If you correct other people's grammar, you might want to refrain from that. If you get teased for being sloppy, why not challenge yourself to change your appearance? If your bully enjoys your reaction of kicking and screaming, try with all your might to ignore him and walk away. Think positively about your situation and accept the challenge! I repeat, it is *not* your fault you are bullied, but if you can work with the situation, then why not try?

You naturally want to fight back, and sometimes it works, but the experts on bullying say that it usually doesn't. Bullies are usually bigger; you might lose and get injured and be worse off than before. Even if you win, the bully might seek revenge. Here's what God says:

- Turn the other cheek (Matt. 5:39).
- Return good for evil (1 Thess. 5:15).
- Love your enemies (Matt. 5:44).
- Vengeance is mine; I will repay (Rom. 12:19).

In other words, be nice to those who are mean to you and don't get back at your bully, because God will. I know this totally goes against what you want to do, but turn the whole business over to God, and just wait to see what He will do.

Of course, there is a place for self-defense. If you are in danger, by all means, try to escape or defend yourself. You might even want to take karate lessons, but only use your skills if necessary. This could also give you more confidence and allow you to vent your frustration, which might help the whole situation.

Girls tend to use words as weapons. If you are being wounded by words, then you need words to heal you. Express your hurt to God, a friend, your mom, a teacher, or your diary. Don't bottle it up; it will foment inside you. Just sharing will help, but others may offer solutions as well. Rachel Simmons, in her book on girls' aggression, advises, "Lose them."[4] If the popular, snotty girls reject you, find friends who accept you and share your interests. Don't keep trying to be "in"; you'll keep feeling lousy. Notice someone else who might not be so noticeable. You might find a very special friend in her.

You need to forgive your bully. "What!" you say. Look at it this way: do you want to carry your bully around with you, like a ball and chain shackled to your ankle? Do you want to be weighed down by him now and into your adult life? Of course not! Then forgive him. If you hang onto the bitterness, it will grow like mold inside you. You're a sinner; he's a sinner. Let him go. Pity him for all the trouble he causes himself and others. Pray for him and release him to God.

If the situation doesn't change or is dangerous, you may need help from adults. He may have threatened you not to tell anyone, but there are people who are stronger than he is. It's not good for him or anybody else for this bullying to continue. Does your school have a system to deal with bullying? Work with the system. Tell your teacher privately or write a letter. If you fear retaliation, ask your teacher to deal carefully with the situation. You might think things are impossible, but adults have options that you might not know about.

And keep praying. God is stronger and wiser than you can even imagine. Ask Him for help; He promises to answer. Be patient and keep praying. He might have a long-term goal in mind for you. Just trust Him.

Be proactive. Don't hide in your room and play video games; you'll be more miserable. Don't hang out with kids who influence you negatively; they'll drag you down deeper. Get out and do something good! Take charge of your situation. What are your interests? What are your strengths?

Make use of the talents God has given you. Read the Bible for help; you'll be amazed at what you'll find. Look around; help someone else. There's nothing like serving others to bring happiness to yourself. John F. Kennedy said, "Ask not what your country can do for you; ask what you can do for your country."[5] You could replace "country" with "school" or "friends."

This struggle seems endless, but it *will* end. Winston Churchill famously urged his hearers never to give in. You know how the roots of trees reach deeper into the earth, searching for water in times of drought. This makes the tree stronger and more able to withstand hardship in the future. If you are being bullied, you are living through a drought of kindness. Reach deeper. Reach for the love of God. Let your roots search for the Living Water, Jesus Christ. That is the only way, and it's the best way, to come out of this whole ordeal richer than before. You will be a much stronger person for going through it.

If you are like Peter

I don't know you, but if you are mean to one or more other people, then I'd like to have a chat with you. This is just a book, so it's safe to be open and honest.

You are not a rock; you're a person who interacts with other people and you have feelings. You want to be happy, right? You want people to treat you with respect or admiration. You usually care what others think of you. You have emotions—happiness, sadness, embarrassment, anger, and satisfaction. Your experiences with other people do have an impact on your life.

You must be completely honest. What kind of a person

are you to others? Are you mean to someone? It's alright to admit it: we've all been mean to others at some point in our lives. That doesn't mean it's okay; it just means we're all sinners. Take a serious look at yourself. What are you doing that is unkind? Do you physically bully someone? Do you intimidate a weaker person? Do you use words to damage someone? You need to get a clear picture of what you are doing. Writing it down might help you understand the situation.

Next, do you know why you bully? Do you understand what makes you do it, what goes through your thoughts at that moment? Are you angry with the person you are bullying? With someone else? Do you feel inadequate in some way, which makes you want to humiliate someone else? Do you want to show how strong you are? How smart? Maybe you are irritated at the person you bully, and you just don't care about him, so you want him out of your way. Maybe you are surrounded by peer pressure that forces you to be tough and mean in order to be cool. Are you bullied by someone else? Maybe you're abused at home. What is your home like? Is violence a part of home life? Is there a lot of yelling in your family? Do you have both a dad and a mom at home or just one parent? Are you taught to control yourself, or do you do as you please? What do you do in your spare time? Do you play video games? Are they violent? What TV shows, internet activities, and music are you into? Do these affect your thoughts and actions positively or negatively? What are your friends like? Are you a leader or a follower? Does the influence of your friends make you bully or be kind to others? If you can't find any reasons, is it simply your personality to be unkind?

The next thing to think about is the person that you bully. We'll call him or her your "victim." You may not think of him that way, but if you are a bully, then you do have a victim. Do you think about how he feels when you bully him? If you mostly think about yourself, please try to understand how your victim feels. This is very important. Put yourself in his place. How would it feel to live in fear? To be miserable at school all day? To be ridiculed? To have no friends? To have people say untrue, unkind things about you? Take a few minutes, sit in a chair, and just imagine what it would be like to be your victim. In your mind, walk through his day. Think about his feelings of fear, dread, pain, embarrassment, sadness, anger, or frustration.

It's probably not too comfortable to feel the feelings of your victim. You might not even realize it, but if you are in the habit of being unkind to someone, you simply cannot be happy, no matter how hard you try to convince yourself that you are. Here's why: it's guilt. When you are mean, your conscience speaks, and that makes you uncomfortable and edgy. Your bullying might give you a feeling of triumph, but it doesn't last. It can't bring you real joy. This makes you want to bully again, to get that triumphant feeling back. Or you may just give in to your anger and frustration and, instead of controlling yourself, you vent it on someone else. It's a vicious cycle, a habit.

"It's just temporary," you say. "I won't act this way as an adult." But you are laying a foundation right now on which the rest of your life is being built. If you keep bullying, you have a five times greater chance of having a criminal record by age 30 than someone who doesn't bully. You are more likely to drop out of school and have a job that doesn't use your skills or pay you for them. You are more likely to abuse your spouse and children.[6] Your future doesn't look great.

Real courage

I would like to challenge you. You've got the energy right now; you just need to change direction. It will take courage. Your friends have come to expect certain behavior from you, and they might give you a hard time. But be strong! Here are some reasons to change.

If you are a guy who wants to come across as tough and macho, then muster up the courage to be kind! Any strong guy can knock over a small guy. That's not courage; that's cowardice. But it takes real strength for a strong guy to defend a weak guy. That's the purpose you were made for![7] Everybody wants to live for a purpose.

If you are a girl who uses words to hurt others, I have a challenge for you as well. If you have been "successful" at bullying, then you must have power with your words. Your friends listen to you. You have an impact on others. Your goal may be to elevate yourself in the eyes of others, but your words are walking you in the wrong direction. Jesus taught that those who serve others will be promoted (Luke 22:26–27). Take an honest look at your motives, find someone to pour your bad feelings out to, and put those negatives behind you—with a lot of prayer and God's almighty power. Then start using the power of your words to heal, to help, and to be kind. You will find much more fulfillment in helping others than you did in hurting them.

Your own happiness is another reason to be kind. If you are in the habit of bullying, you don't even realize that you are missing the joy that kindness brings. Give it a try. Start small or start big. Take the neighbor's garbage out. Speak an encouraging word to someone who's down. Help your little sister with her homework. Do the dishes for your mom when she's not expecting it. Just do some nice things and see how it makes you feel valuable.

There was once a high school student who was hooked on marijuana. He had to do some service work for a class, so he helped deliver Thanksgiving baskets. This school's volunteer group would place the basket on the front steps, ring the doorbell, hide in the bushes, and watch the people's reaction. After seeing the joy he helped bring to needy families, he said, "That's the best high I've ever had!"[8]

Improving your reputation is another reason to be kind. You might be popular with your peers, but you know that some people don't trust you. Your past behavior makes the adults who know you watch you carefully and avoid giving you responsibilities. By changing the direction of your life, you will be given more opportunities that could lead to lifelong success. It will take time, so be patient and stick with it.

Here is a very important reason to be kind: you don't like being miserable, so why bring misery to someone else? Get rid of selfishness. Take your victim's pain and make it your own. Then you will be a much nicer person. Others will like you better, and so will you.

Each of us has some characteristic that's not "normal": perhaps a big nose, weird toes, low intelligence in some area, a squeaky voice. But what's "normal"? Why not enjoy the variety that God created in the human race, and appreciate people for who they are? Mocking people for their personal characteristics hurts deeply and causes scars that last a life-time. Do you really want to wound in such a way?

It goes back to the Golden Rule—treat others the way you want to be treated. Jesus knew that each of us would stand up for our own rights, so He taught us to pull up our neighbor right next to ourselves on our platform. It's simple; ask yourself, "How would I want to be treated?" Then do precisely that for someone else.

But the most important reason to be kind is this: God hates bullying. He sees it and He's keeping track. The Book of Proverbs lists seven things that God hates, and each one can be a form of bullying, directly or indirectly. They are: looking (and acting) proud, lying, hurting an innocent person, thinking up evil plans, being eager to do bad things, slandering others, and stirring up trouble between people (Prov. 6:16–19). God made you and He has the right to expect good behavior. He also has the power to destroy you at any moment. You are living dangerously.

God's hatred for evil is strong, but His passion for protecting the weak is even stronger. During His three years of public ministry, to whom did Jesus reach out? To those who were sick, handicapped, sinful, weak, insane, and poor. Kindness and compassion were His trademarks. God is on the side of needy people; you really ought to be, too (Ps. 90:8, 11; Luke 10:30–37).

I hope you are persuaded. I know that change won't be easy. You might need to change your surroundings. Look for a strong mentor, possibly a youth leader, pastor, teacher, parent, friend, or neighbor. Maybe you need a new batch of friends. If you are spending a lot of time on video games or other media that influence you negatively, change the diet of your entertainment. Join a group or a club that does positive things that you are interested in. It will make a huge difference. Surround yourself with good influences and expect good things to happen. But don't go at it alone; ask for God's power. Pray often. Read the Bible to find answers and gain wisdom. Only then will you be equipped for the battle.

All of us

It would be great if nobody bullied. But that's not enough. Being a "good person" isn't even enough. We are all sinners. Bullies, victims, and everybody in between. And we are heading to hell unless someone intervenes. That someone is Jesus Christ. He is the Son of God the Father, and He left the comfort of His heavenly home to live on this earth for thirty-three years, never sinning once, yet taking the punishment of hell for sinners like you and me. He sincerely offers His salvation to you and me.

When you ask for food from your parents, they don't give you rocks or snakes. If your parents, who are sinners, give you good things, how much more so will God, who is perfect, give the Holy Spirit to those that ask (Luke 11:10–13)? Jesus spoke in simple terms, "If ye shall ask any thing in my name, I will do it" (John 14:14). We must repent of our sins and believe in the Lord Jesus Christ (Mark 1:15, Acts 16:31).

Imagine you committed a series of crimes. You robbed, you destroyed, and you murdered. You are arrested, tried, pronounced guilty on all charges, and sentenced to death. During the time you are awaiting trial, a friend counsels you and convinces you of how bad your acts of crime were. As you hear your sentence, your head droops. You say how sorry you are, knowing you fully deserve the punishment. But wait! Your friend is there, and he steps up to the podium. He says, "I will take his place. He can go free, and I will die for him, because I love him." You can hardly believe such good news. There is even better news than that. It is the gospel. And Jesus Christ did that and more. He takes the mess that we have made of our lives, opens our eyes to see how bad we are, and makes us new creatures. Ask Him and keep asking Him until you receive an answer: "Lord, show me Thy power, change my life, give me love for Thee and for other people, give me repentance, and give me faith. Make me a child of the King."

1. Joel R. Beeke and Diana Kleyn, *How God Sent A Dog To Save A Family* (Grand Rapids, Mich.: Reformation Heritage Books, 2003), 85–91.

2. Frank Peretti, *No More Victims* (Nashville, Tenn.: Nelson Impact, 2001), 43.

3. Ibid., 47.

4. Rachel Simmons, *Odd Girl Out* (San Diego: Harcourt, Inc., 2002), 256–257.

5. John F. Kennedy, Inaugural Address, January 20, 1961.

6. L. Rowell Huesmann, Jessica Moise-Titus, Cheryl-Lynn Podolski, and Leonard Eron, "Longitudinal Relations Between Children's Exposure to TV Violence and Their Aggressive and Violent Behavior in Young Adulthood: 1977–1992," *Developmental Psychology* 39, no. 2 (March, 2003), 201–221.

7. Frank Peretti, *No More Victims* (Nashville, Tenn.: Nelson Impact, 2001), 55.

8. Interview with Jay Eveland, Student Volunteer Coordinator, East Kentwood High School, Kentwood, Michigan.

PART 3
Kindness in Action

CHAPTER 10
Kind Thoughts

THE COOKIE THIEF
Valerie Cox

A woman was waiting at an airport one night,
With several long hours before her flight,
She hunted for a book in the airport shop,
Bought a bag of cookies and found a place to drop.
She was engrossed in her book, but happened to see,
That the man sitting beside her, as bold as could be,
Grabbed a cookie or two from the bag between,
Which she tried to ignore, to avoid a scene.
She read, munched cookies, and watched the clock,
As the gutsy "cookie thief" diminished her stock.
She was getting more irritated as the minutes ticked by,
Thinking, "If I wasn't so nice, I would blacken his eye!"
With each cookie she took, he took one too.
When only one was left, she wondered what he'd do.
With a smile on his face and a nervous laugh,
He took the last cookie and broke it in half.
He offered her half, as he ate the other.
She snatched it from him and thought, Oh brother,
This guy has some nerve and he's also rude.
Why, he didn't even show any gratitude!

She had never known when she had been so galled,
And sighed with relief when her flight was called.
She gathered her belongings and headed to the gate,
Refusing to look back at the "thieving ingrate."
She boarded the plane and sank in her seat,
Then sought her book, which was almost complete.
As she reached in her baggage, she gasped with surprise:
There were her cookies in front of her eyes.
If mine are here, she moaned with despair,
Then the others were his and he tried to share!
Too late to apologize, she realized with grief,
That she was the rude one, the ingrate, the thief![1]

Have you ever done this? You were sure you had a situation
sized up accurately, only to find out later that you were
missing essential information which changed the picture
completely. I have. In fact, I wonder if you and I do this
every day. Maybe multiple times a day.

Is the door open? The door of our minds, that is. Let's
picture each of our minds as a room. We see life through
the windows. Our experiences of childhood and adulthood
are recorded on our walls. The structure of our room is
our personality and the temperament we were born with.
The floor is our foundation of beliefs and attitudes. New
information enters through our door. From our room we
interpret our world.

Whenever we interact with other human beings, we
converse with them, we observe them, and we draw conclusions about them and about the events surrounding them.
Our way of thinking and our past experiences affect our
assessment of a situation. It happens millions of times a day

around the world. It's part of life. But there is a foundation, a philosophy of life, on which each of us bases our judgments. It can be the shaky foundation of human reasoning or it can be the solid foundation of the Word of God.

The foundation of our thoughts

God's creation is bursting with variety: insects that sting, burrow, and fly; birds that fly, walk, and swim; fish that swim, dive, and jump; animals that jump, burrow, and bite; plants that snap, blossom, and nourish. And all these appear in a mind-boggling variety of colors, shapes, and sizes. Variety really is the spice of life.

This same diversity is seen in human beings. Most of us have the same parts: two eyes, one nose, ten each of fingers and toes, two each of arms and legs, a body. Yet no one is exactly the same. What an incredible array of size, color, and physical characteristics we have. Our personalities add more variety. Then we have different experiences, which mold us and make us who we are. What is the big picture? Millions of unique individuals, all designed by the same Creator.

What does this have to do with kind thoughts? It means that, whenever we have interactions with others or simply observe them, our underlying premise ought to be, "There goes another variation of the human race. He looks and acts different from me. But God created both of us. We are both sinners who need to be saved. He has the same value as I do. I love my neighbor as myself. The diversity in God's creation is beautiful and interesting." From there, we can start making interpretations.

Tolerance, diversity, love, open-mindedness: these are the buzzwords today of those who are politically correct.

But Jesus practiced these principles long before the modern day adherents did. He tolerated the insane and cared for them enough to heal them. He accepted diverse groups of people, shown by His eating with swindling tax collectors and public sinners. He showed love to the lepers by restoring their health. He was open-minded enough to bless the little children when others didn't want to bother with them.

There are differences, of course. The modernists tolerate almost any religious belief, though they don't give much breathing space to Christianity. Their promotion of diversity and open-mindedness shuts down when values of right and wrong are discussed. And love lasts as long as the topic of sin is not brought up.

Jesus' parameters were clear and fair. He said, as it were, "I created you. You sinned. I despise sin because I am holy. You deserve to be punished, but I sincerely offer My own life to pay for your sins. If you reject Me, it is your own doing, and you will end up in hell. If you repent of your sins and believe on Me, I will save you, and you will see that I changed your heart. I am the God of love, and you will become a truly loving person who loves what is good."

God is very patient with people who rebel against Him, much more patient than we would be. He waits and He offers salvation. But His patience will eventually run out. Then it will be death, destruction, and hell. He loves to show mercy, but because He is perfectly holy, His anger against evil will prevail. It is this foundation of God's mercy and justice on which we base our thoughts. Jesus' example and teachings are replete with valuable wisdom.

Signposts for kind thoughts

As we travel life's pathway, there are certain signposts that will direct us down the road of kindness. They are humility, empathy and compassion, discernment, and love.

Humility

A plaque in the gift store read, "The whole world is a little bit weird, except you and me. And then sometimes I even wonder about you." Do you ever detect that attitude in yourself? I certainly have my days. But who even has the final say on what "weird" is? Instead of thinking of that elderly lady who wears an antique hat and white gloves and who talks to the birds as just a little strange, why not enjoy her as an interesting part of God's incredible creation?

Personally, I really like unique people. They expand my horizons, I often learn something from them, and I find it refreshing to meet people who buck normalcy without defying God. If everybody were normal, life would be rather boring. It is extraordinarily interesting to talk with people and learn what is special about them.

Our unkind thoughts often stem from pride. "I would never do something like that," we say. That may be true, but the bottom line is that we are all sinners; we just come in different varieties.

Sometimes the faults we see so clearly in others are precisely the ones we house in our own bodies. The reason we recognize these sins is because we are so familiar with them ourselves. Psychologists call this "projection." The thief thinks his neighbor is stealing from him. The gossiper accuses her friend of destroying her reputation. If we truly

understand ourselves and our own shortcomings, we will
be humble.

Paul noticed the human tendency toward pride and
urged the Philippians, "In lowliness of mind, let each esteem other better than themselves" (Phil. 2:3). He explained
how we must have the same thoughts as Jesus did who was
sinless God, yet who "made himself of no reputation, and
took upon him the form of a servant, and was made in the
likeness of men" (Phil. 2:7). That is great humility—to be
God and to become a servant. But He did more. He died a
humiliating death on the cross so that death-deserving sinners like us can live. If perfect Jesus can become a humble
servant, then certainly imperfect you and I should walk
humbly with our fellow-sinners. Whatever goodness is
found in us is simply a gift from God; we can't take credit
for it. To paraphrase the sixteenth-century English Re-
former John Bradford, when he saw a criminal on his way
to his execution, "There but for the grace of God go I."[2]

Often we think of other people in terms of deservedness
or worthiness. "Derek wronged me, so I won't help him
out of his misery." "Natasha's pretty popular; maybe I'll
help her with her work in order to be her friend." Do
we subconsciously place a value on others in relation to
ourselves and then proceed to think kindly of them—or
not so kindly? Scripture answers, "Put on therefore, as the
elect of God, holy and beloved, bowels of mercies, kindness,
humbleness of mind, meekness, longsuffering" (Col. 3:12).
Lest we think some neighbors do not deserve our kind
thoughts, Jesus answers our protests, "But love ye your
enemies, and do good, and lend, hoping for nothing again;
and your reward shall be great, and ye shall be the children

of the Highest: for he is kind unto the unthankful and to the evil" (Luke 6:35).

James specifically warns against partiality (James 2:1–9). He describes two men entering a gathering. One is a rich man dressed in very nice clothing and fine jewelry, and the other is a poor man dressed in filthy clothing. If we give favorable attention to the rich man and reject the poor man, we are judging in a way that goes contrary to the royal law, which is to love our neighbor as ourselves. The truly kind person has a sense of fairness and esteems every person to be a valuable creature of God's creation.

Empathy and compassion

We are called to show compassion to our fellowman. "Rejoice with them that do rejoice, and weep with them that weep" (Rom. 12:15). "Bear ye one another's burdens, and so fulfill the law of Christ" (Gal. 6:2). Picture the poignant scene of Jesus standing by the grave of Lazarus, seeing the grief of friends and family. What did He do? Jesus wept. We too must enter into the thoughts and feelings of our neighbor and then ask, "What can I do to lift his load?" Maybe a fitting word will give a cancer victim the courage for one more chemo treatment. A hug, a touch, or a smile can say, "I understand. I've been there." Assistance in the form of food, clothing, or money can offer kindness and relief. Big or small, we are called to care.

Discernment

"But are we supposed to love just anybody, without regard for whether they are doing right or wrong?" you might say. Not at all. Jesus warns us not to sin, nor to enter situations of temptation. He said, "Wherefore by their fruits ye shall know them" (Matt. 7:20). We must be discerning in order to protect ourselves from evil, but we can still show kindness and love to those who are not walking in God's ways, in order to try to lead them to the Lord.

The Bible also says, "Judge not, that ye be not judged" (Matt. 7:1). This frequently misinterpreted text does not contradict Matthew 7:20. It addresses rash judgment, as when we make conclusions without knowing all the facts, when we judge someone's motives incorrectly, or when we publicize private wrongdoings. These verses condemn hypocritical judging. Jesus asks why you or I would criticize a neighbor for the splinter in his eye when we can't even see well because of the beam that is in our own eye. We must focus on cleaning up our own sins before trying to purify others. When we do this, it's quite likely we will become humble enough to quit judging unjustly altogether.

Love

As water soaks the soil around a plant, then wends its way through the roots, the stem, the branches, and finally to the leaves, so love is the life source that nourishes our kind thoughts. With love, we will have humility, empathy, and discernment. We will flourish with the peace and joy that accompanies a philosophy of kindness, and we will nourish others with the fruits that will inevitably follow. With love in our hearts, the line between my happiness and my neighbor's happiness will blur. We multiply each other's joys and divide our burdens. "And above all these things put on charity [steadfast love], which is the bond of perfectness" (Col. 3:14).

Day to day

The fruits will follow. Kind thoughts can't help but be shown by kind actions. Rather than having "cookie thief" experiences, we will find ourselves offering cookies to our neighbor. Let's open the doors of our minds, try to avoid leaping to wrong conclusions, and think kind thoughts. Here are some day-to-day examples.

I knew a man who was married and had five children. He had a job for a while but was relegated to part-time, and then he could not hold a job at all. He was an added responsibility for his wife to care for. From all outside observations, he was not worthy of much respect. But there is a story behind him. This man served our country in World War II. In one battle, his company attacked the enemy by marching off a boat onto land. The first wave of soldiers was shot down. So was the second. He was in the third wave. As he stepped over dead bodies, he recognized them as his comrades, and five decades later he could still tell their names to his son. He survived—at least physically. After traumatic battles, he'd be pulled out and given Thorazine pills to block the memories. This would knock him out for two days; then he would be put into the fray again. He received no hero's welcome when he returned home. He always felt he did a poor job. And the memories weren't erased. Shell shock, they called it then. Post-traumatic stress disorder is what they call it now. But he had a heart of gold; he would give the shirt off his back to anyone in need, his son remembers. He did odd jobs at home and for others. God gave him a diligent, committed wife and cheerful, energetic children who took up the slack, cared for him, loved him, and learned to understand the disabled. Is the door of my mind open when I think of him or other veterans? When I see the homeless, do I remember that a high percentage of them are veterans? How would you and I have reacted had we experienced what they did?

Studies have shown that different individuals have different levels of pain tolerance. You see it in children. The tough little two-year-old boy goes skidding on his belly through the dirt, gets up, and keeps chasing that snake, ignoring his bloody scrapes. But the skinny, soft, little girl in pink ruffles cries when her skin is barely scratched. They simply have different pain tolerances. You and I don't have a wire into other peoples' brains. Sometimes we really don't feel their pain. Is my mind open to believe that they really are in pain?

"Tom" is middle-aged. He is very friendly, but he makes people uncomfortable sometimes by getting too close, and he can get violently angry at unexpected times. He, too, has a story. When he was younger he had a serious accident that resulted in severe head injuries, and he was in a coma for an extended period of time. He lived and has made incredible gains with therapy, but the effects of the closed head injury will never leave him. He loves the Lord and he loves people, but he can't always control his impulses. How do we think of people with mental or emotional difficulties? Judgmentally or with acceptance? Do we avoid them or are we friendly to them? They are often acutely aware that they are "different," but they want to be treated normally. Let's take a lesson from the kind souls who work with these people and call them "special." And not just *call* them special, but also *think* of them in that way, and treat them in a special way.

A teenage son forgot to bring his musical instrument home for practice. The same evening, he remembered at bedtime that he had a paper due the next morning. His mom accused him of slacking, but she forgot that he had improved his efforts over the last two months. We sometimes zero in on our children's failures with microscopic vision because that is what catches our attention and gets in our way. Meanwhile, we don't notice the big picture. The boy is basically a good kid; he is just a "work in progress."

Spouses might be further along in the growing process, but with them, too, we do well to look at the big picture, be careful about judging motives, avoid microscopic examination, and emphasize the positive in him or her. After all, that's the treatment we wish for from others, and aren't we all works in progress?

Do you have a family in your church, school, or neighborhood who has many problems—problems like physical illness, mental illness, financial problems, work problems, problems with personal relationships, or any combination of these? Such personal difficulties might affect the larger community, especially a church, by necessitating that fellow members help continually, sacrificing time, money, and effort. Have we ever caught ourselves judging these friends, wondering if they have brought their problems on themselves somehow, trying to see a reason within them, blaming them? Are we like Job's friends, "helping" by enlightening them about the sins for which God must be punishing them?

It is quite possible our judgments are correct, at least in part. But is it possible that God has a double purpose? Is He testing us as well? Could it be that God is looking over our shoulder and into our heart, saying, "I've put this individual and this family in your midst. Are you going to help them with their problems short-term and long-term? Will you persevere with them the way I persevere with you, even though they are sinners?"

One day, I was picking my raspberries. I was in a hurry, so I only picked them from two sides, but I was sure I had gotten them all. Later on, while I was picking tomatoes, I noticed I had missed some raspberries. I looked at the bushes from different angles, lifted leaves, looked under the branches, and found many more. I am afraid that is how we judge situations sometimes. Though we only know a few facts, we think we know all the facts, and we proceed to make a judgment. Only later do we find out there are more facts that change the whole picture.

Fruit and thorns

Those raspberries have prickly stalks. We can choose to focus on the sweet, beautiful fruit, or we can say, "I don't like that whole bush because of its thorny stem." Likewise, we can observe people and focus on their positive traits, or we can simply dismiss them as inferior because of their thorns. With the law of kindness written on our hearts, we will see the berries more than the thorns and we will have a heart of compassion for our fellow-sinners. We will realize that they may change with time. We will realize we probably don't know all the facts and we might be making a wrong conclusion, or we may acknowledge that we don't even need to know the whole story.

Of course, there are some people who produce little or no fruit, and whose thorns are painfully prominent.

We can still be humble, empathetic, compassionate, discerning, and loving towards them. And we can pray. We can pray that the Almighty God will help them and change them. Instead of looking down on that rebellious teen, we can be friendly to him and pray for his conversion. Rather than judging that unorganized mom for not watching her kids, we can pray for their safety and lend a hand. Instead of scurrying past the homeless person, we can give them a tract, a gift certificate to McDonald's, and a smile. Rather than being disgusted with the immodest clothing of the teenage neighbor girl, we might realize she is looking for the male approval she isn't getting at home, befriend her, and pray she doesn't walk down the wrong pathway in life. When we meet someone who is critical of everybody, we might realize he may have been cruelly criticized as a child. If someone's phone is busy all day, we can't assume they are talking endlessly. Maybe they are sick or the phone is off the hook by mistake. Let's color our conclusions with compassion.

Every day affords us endless opportunity for misunderstandings or for being understanding. Which path will we take? After Jesus tells us to love our enemies in Luke 6, He continues with instruction to guide our thoughts. But He doesn't stop with telling us to do the right thing. There are also rewards! His words are a fitting conclusion. "Be ye therefore merciful, as your Father also is merciful. Judge not, and ye shall not be judged: condemn not, and ye shall not be condemned: forgive, and ye shall be forgiven: Give, and it shall be given unto you; good measure, pressed down, and shaken together, and running over, shall men give into your bosom. For with the same measure that ye mete withal it shall be measured to you again" (Luke 6:36–38).

---

1. Valerie Cox, copyright, "The Cookie Thief" in *A Third Serving of Chicken Soup for the Soul*, ed. Jack Canfield and Mark Victor Hansen (Deerfield Beach, Fla.: Health Communications, 1996), 199–200.

2. John Bartlett, *Familiar Quotations*, ed. Emily Morison Beck, 14th ed. (Boston: Little, Brown, 1968), 186.

CHAPTER 11

Kind Words

⟨ ⟩

"Sticks and stones can break my bones, but words can never hurt me." Certain truisms are not true. Could the opposite be true?

Sticks and stones can break my bones,
Six weeks in a cast, the pain is gone.
But those words still burn; my eyes fill with tears,
And the scars live on and on and on through the years.

We've all been touched by the power of words, for better or for worse. From birth they have molded us. A mother's loving words are the building blocks of relationships. Instructive words of parents and teachers prepare us for the future. Abusive words can break us down or make us stronger. The words we hear as adults have the power to make us happy, sad, satisfied, angry, afraid, or relieved. Words impact our lives in a huge way.

Just how powerful are words? James compares the tongue (our words) to the small rudder that is able to turn a large ship in the face of fierce winds. The tongue is very small, yet it can make big boasts. It can start large fires. Without God's grace, much sin happens with our words. Only God's grace can truly tame the tongue and make

our words pure, peaceable, gentle, merciful, and without
partiality or hypocrisy (James 3).

Scripture is replete with verses on this topic. Here are
several clear principles. First, communication is important.
God has communicated with man since creation. It was
beautiful then, but it became marred by the fall in Paradise.
Yet in God's infinite kindness, His words told us the good
news of the gospel. His words opened the door to a fresh,
new start. Today we have *the written Word*, the Bible, which
is our guide for life. We, in turn, answer God with our
prayers. We express the innermost feelings of our heart.
God-man communication is necessary.

Person-to-person communication is vital as well. We
convey information to each other, we express our emotions,
we relay events, we learn and teach, and we discuss
plans. Words are the substance of relationships. There is
wonderful variety among us in the quantity of words we
utter and the style we employ.[1]

Another principle is that sin underlies our words. It is
too bad we have to keep referring to sin, but the reality is
that we are sinners. Our hearts are sinful. The words that
flow from our hearts are sinful words. By understanding this
and the nature of our sinful words, we can fight temptation
and become more positive, kinder, and more loving with
our words, God helping us.

There are bad words and there are good words. We
can divide words into these simplistic categories, though
in real life the categories easily become muddled. I would
define bad words as those that hurt people, that do damage
in relationships, that dishonor God or my neighbor, or that
are not profitable. Good words honor and love God and my

neighbor, they have a positive effect on others, they are true and kind, or they serve a good purpose. Good words have the power to heal individuals and relationships.

Unkind words

Words take on many forms. Demeaning words strike like a dagger into the heart: "Why can't you do this simple task? You'll never amount to anything when you grow up." Weed-seeds of gossip are blown in the wind and take root in the minds of those who hear them: "I heard he used drugs when he was younger. That's probably why he's so lazy now." Words can have a cold, wet blanket effect: "You got an A? It must have been an easy test."

Gossip, slander, backbiting, boasting, lies, threats, unnecessary complaints, flattery, and mockery are all negative words. Other examples are unkind, conspiring, foolish, angry, sarcastic, idle, and argumentative words. Even positive words, such as "That's great!" spoken in a sarcastic tone of voice can hurt. An absence of words can also injure, as seen in the stony silence of passive-aggressive behavior.

Cruel and destructive words

David had extensive experience with enemies. He accused Doeg in Psalm 52:2-4 of using his words like a sharp razor to devise mischief and to work deceit. Doeg loved evil more than good and lying rather than speaking righteousness, and he loved all devouring words. David described the speech of the evil person in Psalm 10:7-9: "His mouth is full of cursing and deceit and fraud: under his tongue is mischief and vanity. He sitteth in the lurking places of the villages: in the secret places doth he murder the innocent: his eyes are privily set against the poor. He lieth in wait secretly as a lion in his den: he lieth in wait to catch the poor: he doth catch the poor, when he draweth him into his net."

Proverbs is very clear about what God hates. Of the seven things listed in Proverbs 6:16–19, three directly involve speech: "a lying tongue,... a false witness that speaketh lies, and he that soweth discord among brethren." Of the remaining four things, speech is often an accessory: "a proud look,... hands that shed innocent blood, an heart that deviseth wicked imaginations, [and] feet that be swift in running to mischief." All seven hateful items involve injury to others. God cares very much whether or not kindness is shown to our neighbor.

But most of us are not criminals pursuing evil or malicious enemies like Doeg. We are decent, law-abiding citizens. We're usually kind to others. That may be true; thank the Lord for that. But are there "little indiscretions" we allow ourselves? I would like to challenge you: Does your speech live up to the standard found in Proverbs? What temptations should you resist with more energy? Do you use your speech for kindness to your neighbor? Let's discuss those "little" things.

Me-boosters

Our motives for speaking negative words could be compared to a see-saw. We put the other person down; we go up. We elevate ourselves; the other person goes down. Either way, we win. Or so it seems. Eventually, it catches up to us, though, depending on how much we ride the see-saw. Many of our negative words are tied to this motive.

The main type of "me-booster" is boasting. Many

children unabashedly and naturally do this. "I'm stronger than you are." "My sweater is prettier than yours." We ought to outgrow this by adulthood, but some of us simply become more sophisticated at it. "I was surprised, but my boss promoted me instead of my colleague. Now I'm glad I put forth so much more effort than him." "I have tried to help her with disciplining her children; after all, my kids turned out fine. But she just won't take my advice." There are two things wrong with boasting. It is the verbal manifestation of pride in the heart, and God doesn't approve of pride. Everything that we have to boast about is from Him. But also, inherent in boasting is comparison with others, and most boasters aren't satisfied with an even playing field. Publicized superiority is the goal. So for one to be up on the see-saw, someone has to be put down. And kindness is usually missing in the scenario.

One irony about boasting is that our words are often true. We figure we are simply stating the facts. But Proverbs 27:2 admonishes, "Let another man praise thee, and not thine own mouth; a stranger, and not thine own lips." In certain settings, as with a best friend or a spouse, we can share the joy of our accomplishments. But pride so easily creeps into our motives and we end up speaking words of self-aggrandizement that would be better left unsaid. In reality, if it is so important, others will eventually find out. We don't really need the attention, do we? It actually works against us ultimately. It is distasteful for adults to boast.

Flattery is a more subtle form of ingratiating speech. We give an untruthful or exaggerated compliment, not for the promotion of our neighbor, but to win their favor and promote ourselves. We might not think this is so bad; after all, nice things are being spoken. But God doesn't tolerate it because He looks beyond the flattery to the heart of the flatterer. What does He see? Deceitfulness (Ps. 12:2–3), an intention to trap or do evil (Prov. 7:5; 29:5), or a desire for personal gain (Jude 16). Flattery feeds the pride of both parties involved for an end that's not good. It's not truthful, and it's not God-honoring.

Flattery is not to be confused with encouragement or praise. There is nothing wrong with giving a truthful compliment for the purpose of being kind. "That outfit looks really pretty on you," can bring cheer. Gratitude is also an expression of humility: "Thanks so much for giving my son a ride. You are a generous person." Where there is love, there is a natural inclination to praise. Remember Proverbs 27:2; it is acceptable for one person to praise another. Just let it be truthful and for an altruistic purpose.

Put-downs

Boasting and flattery elevate me; gossip, slander, tattling, mocking, and bullying are put-downs to you. Gossip and slander are closely related. A gossip is "a person who chatters or repeats idle talk and rumors, especially about the private affairs of others."[2] Slander inflicts more injury. It is "the utterance in the presence of another person of a false statement, damaging to a third person's character or reputation."[3] Gossip may or may not be true—often it is a mixture—but slander is false. The motive of the gossip is sometimes innocent, sometimes malicious, and sometimes mixed. The slanderer's motives are malicious. Both can do irreparable damage to another person's reputation.

"George" is a church leader. He and his wife "Matilda"

and a group of concerned parents from their church attended a seminar presented by a conservative Christian organization on the temptations that young people face in today's culture. Most of the seminar was verbal instruction and a small part was visual. It was a realistic presentation, meant to alert unenlightened parents to the sordid influence of the media on their teens. One of the parents, "Harriet," sat next to Matilda and smiled and whispered often with George and Matilda during the presentation. Several weeks later, a rumor circulated to the effect that George enjoyed seeing the pictures at the seminar. Other members of the church leadership were appalled and questioned him vigorously. As it turned out, Harriet had watched George during the presentation and concluded that he derived pleasure from what he saw. She then shared her assessment with other church leaders, who were eager to believe her. One elder spread a rumor throughout a number of churches that George was going to places to engage in pornographic activity. Harriet's gossip was a mixture of truth and distortion. George did watch the few, somewhat graphic pictures—as did the entire audience—but his reaction was not one of pleasure; he was asking, "How can we protect our youth from this danger?" By spreading and exaggerating gossip to the point of falsehood, Harriet and the elder compromised George's reputation.

"Sally" thought she was happily married, but her husband, "Leonard," suddenly left her. She found out later it was for another woman. She found a job to support herself and her three young sons. It was only the Lord's hand of providence and His tender love that upheld her as she poured every ounce of energy into her children and her job.

Meanwhile, her husband totally shed his Christianity, went from wife to wife, and did not show up to give time, love, or support to his children. Decades later, when the boys had families of their own, Leonard began to correspond with them. By gradually chipping away at the good reputation of their mother, by distorting facts, by lying that he had tried to contact them but was hindered by her, he actually turned their hearts away from their mother and toward himself. He capitalized on the big, empty spots in the hearts of these boys who needed their dad, and he had no qualms about lying. This man was a slanderer.

Tattling seems to be confined to childhood. When I taught second grade, I had to have a clear understanding of what tattling was. On one hand, I wanted to hear reports of wrongdoing, especially from the playground, where secret corners are shielded from the eyes of the playground patroller. Bullying thrives in the shadows. On the other hand, it wasn't good for certain children to be trying to get others in trouble and making themselves seem better. Tattling, then, pertains not only to the misdeed, but also to the motive of the reporter. Children need an explanation of the difference between necessary reporting and tattling. I would tell the children, "When you see some wrongdoing, check your motive first. If you just want to get the person in trouble and it's something little, let it go. If it's something that needs to be dealt with, talk to the person yourself. If you are afraid, tell the playground patroller, but do it in a concerned way—not gloating, nor with pride in yourself. If you report trouble far more than other people do, you might just be a tattler." Teachers and parents need to address each situation in an individualized manner.

Wounding words have the power to devastate a soul. Unkindness is unleashed in mocking, bullying, and some teasing. This subject is covered in Chapter 8.

After riding the see-saw of me-boosters and put-downs, we have arrived at another group of negative words: those that stem from allowing the gate of our lips to stay open, giving voice to unrestrained, negative emotions within.

Uncontrolled words

A soldier is a picture of strength. He would be a rare and extremely powerful soldier who could conquer a whole city. Yet Solomon says that the person who controls his own spirit is even stronger (Prov. 16:32). Likewise, a person who doesn't exercise self-control is like a broken-down city without walls (Prov. 25:28). When we don't control ourselves, many negative words can spew from our mouths. They appear in the form of complaining and uncontrolled words.

The teenager, standing in front of her full closet, says, "I don't have anything to wear." The grocery store clerk says, "I can't wait to get out of here." The friend you meet in the store says, "Can you believe this weather? It's sweltering"—then, a few months later, "I can't stand this cold, dreary winter." A mom says to her kids, "You guys never clean your rooms." The kids say, "I don't like this food." We are spoiled here in twenty-first-century North America. I've been told it's different in poorer countries, that those with far fewer material goods appear just as happy despite their simpler lifestyles. When we stray from walking closely with the Lord, we forget to count our blessings and acknowledge God who gave them to us.

He sometimes needs to discipline us by taking a privilege away or sending a trial. It gets our attention and we fly back to Him, hoping never to complain again.

Complaints about others often stem from what we perceive as their inadequacies when, in reality, the inadequacies are our own. The lazy person sees others as lazy. The thief thinks everybody wants to steal from him. When we complain, our self-centeredness obscures our vision, and we say unkind things to and about others.

A carpenter's rule is "measure twice, cut once." Maybe we should all practice "think twice, speak once." You can't undo a wrong cut or wrong words. "In the multitude of words there wanteth not sin: but he that refraineth his lips is wise" (Prov. 10:19). The more we speak, the more likely we are to sin. Most of us would be wise to speak less.

Our attitudes can steer our lives. When we nurture a spirit of discontentment in ourselves, we don't like ourselves, we find fault in others, and we see our circumstances as unsatisfactory. Thus we spiral ever deeper into unhappiness. But the same circumstances look much better when our attitude says, "This is God's providence in my life, and I will work to improve things. I am to love God above all and my neighbor as myself. I will depend on the Lord for all things. And I realize I am a sinner who doesn't deserve the blessings I have. If Paul and Silas could sing in the prison, can't I rejoice in my circumstances?" Proverbs 15:15 states, "All the days of the afflicted are evil: but he that is of a merry heart hath a continual feast."

Strife and arguing
During spring, the rains fall. As the water drains, it washes

debris into the stream, then into the river. Sometimes a whirlpool forms, and Styrofoam cups, chunks of wood, and plastic wrappers swirl around in the murky water, hitting each other in uncontrolled fashion before finally washing downstream. It's an environment of strife. People have their whirlpools, too, at home, at work, or in the community. Unkindness abounds in arguing and strife, and anger is often an ingredient as well.

Samuel was an intense boy who had to start sharing at age three, when soft, meek sister Sophie entered the family scene. From that time on, it seemed that things weren't fair. His parents appeared more concerned about protecting Sophie's possessions than permitting Sam to borrow them. They worried about her physical safety when he wanted to wrestle with her. Even when he kissed her, they said he was too rough. He could do no right and she could do no wrong. This perception was reinforced every time his mom got irritated with him. Sam wasn't allowed to show defiance to his parents, so he began to take his frustrations out on Sophie. He poked her, teased her, and looked for things to argue about with her. She learned to defend herself with sarcasm and retaliation. As they grew up, they seemed to hate each other. When they were in the same vicinity, there was often strife.

There are three factors that are present in a situation of strife: circumstances, instigator(s), and selfishness. The circumstances of an argument can be concrete, such as the value of an object being sold, or whose fault an accident was. Or the circumstances can be subtle. Sam's perception was that Sophie was the favored child and that he was cheated. His jealousy colored every interaction with her. Circumstances are always a part of strife, but more influential is the character of the instigator.

There are many varieties of instigators. They were around when Solomon wrote Proverbs, and we still meet them today. There is the angry instigator. "A wrathful man stirreth up strife: but he that is slow to anger appeaseth strife" (Prov. 15:18). Anger is the stirring stick that provokes people, heats up the argument, and makes both parties act in ways they regret later. Revenge is a close relative of anger.

Righteous indignation is not to be confused with sinful anger. God's anger against sin is recorded dozens of times in the Old Testament. Jesus became angry when he witnessed lack of compassion (Mark 10:13–14) and desecration of God's house (Matt. 21:12–13). Paul instructed us, "Be ye angry, and sin not." If it's for God's glory it's not sin, but it should be brief, so that we do not "give place to the devil" (Eph. 4:26–27).

The hateful instigator despises what he sees in others, causing him to focus on the negatives rather than realizing that he is a sinner himself and humbly overlooking others' faults. "Hatred stirreth up strifes: but love covereth all sins" (Prov. 10:12).

Foolishness, pride, and scorn are interwoven in Proverbs. A primary characteristic of a foolish person is that he doesn't listen to advice because he is too proud to believe someone else. He thinks he knows it all, which makes him look foolish—confirming what's inside. When the discussion doesn't go his way, he can't back down, and strife ensues. "Only by pride cometh contention: but with the well advised is wisdom" (Prov. 13:10). Proverbs 18:6 explains how a fool's lips get him into arguments and bring him punishment. Scorn goes one step further: it is pride plus contempt or disdain. "Cast out the scorner, and contention shall go out; yea, strife and reproach shall cease" (Prov. 22:10).

"He is just looking for trouble." Have you ever met anyone like that? I don't mean cute, Dennis-the-Menace mischievousness. I mean devious troublemakers. Scripture describes them as foolish, contentious, meddling, or froward. These people take pleasure in causing pain in others by their words or deeds. They look for strife and enter into it with joy. They claim victory when others are hurt. God doesn't think they're cute; in fact, He hates their behavior (Prov. 6:16–19). The result of this type of behavior is compared to a continual dripping in a very rainy day (Prov. 27:15), adding wood to a fire (Prov. 26:21), wringing someone's nose until it bleeds (Prov. 30:33), and taking a dog by the ears (Prov. 26:17).

If there is any instigator on whom we can have compassion, it is the one who was abused or injured emotionally or physically. When I worked in a psychiatric hospital, the worst cases I observed were those people who had been sexually abused as a child. They are scarred for life. Drug abuse also does devastating damage to the mind. These victims are not always rational. They may bottle up emotions and blow up over issues that would not ruffle most people. Head-injury victims and those with other physical or mental disabilities can also cause strife in society. These individuals may need counseling and medication as well as our love, understanding, and helping hands.

Disagreement between individuals doesn't have to lead to strife. Discussion, compromise, and civility can accomplish much. Picture two people climbing a mountain, disagreeing on an issue. The higher they go, the more intense the discussion becomes. They arrive at the lip of a roiling, red-hot volcanic crater. They turn to each other and say, "Should we add anger and aggravation to our discussion and jump in?" Wisely, they say, "No, let's walk down the peaceful side of this mountain and work it out. The damage will be far less." I believe that with humility, selflessness, generosity, love, forgiveness, prayer, and the Lord's blessing, nearly any situation can be worked out somehow, including business dealings. I don't find any place in Scripture that gives justification for two wise, godly people to have strife between them.

Returning to the whirlpool of strife, the logs and debris crashing around are the circumstances, and the forceful current is the instigator. The third factor, the murky sediment, is ugly selfishness clouding up the whole scene. When we zero in on our own needs and wants, to the exclusion of promoting the well-being of our neighbor, then we are more likely to cause strife. The weed of selfishness chokes out the Golden Rule. On the other hand, if our hearts are inclined to show lovingkindness to others, for their benefit, then the waterways of our lives will flow as a gentle stream, clear and peaceful, bringing life and cheer to all we touch.

Kind words

"A word fitly spoken is like apples of gold in pictures of silver" (Prov. 25:11). Gold and silver? Are words really that valuable? God's Word says they are. If that's the case, we have the ability to bestow great riches on others, no matter how poor we are! What exciting opportunities await us! Our definition again is this: good words honor and love God and my neighbor, they have a positive effect on others, they are true and kind, or they serve a good purpose. Good words have the power to heal individuals and relationships.

Oil flows from an oil well. A mountain stream produces fresh water. The source gives of its own product. A loving heart produces loving words. Some fountains trickle, some effuse. Whether we speak much or little, let our words be good and kind.

Love has tenderness for the loved one. Love wants what is best for the loved one. Love wants to speak lovingly. Love cares about others and wants to serve. Love wants to help when help is needed. We have a deeper love for those who are close to us, and we have a friendship type of love for acquaintances. Several other key ingredients also need to reside in our hearts in order for our words to be kind. They are empathy, appreciation, and humility.

Add empathy to love, and even more kindness happens. The combination of observing a person's situation, putting ourselves in his place, caring about him, understanding his emotions, figuring out if we can help, then saying kind words, is a sequence that is like "apples of gold in pictures of silver" (Prov. 25:11). If we have the law of kindness in our hearts, then we aim to color all our actions and words with kindness—from the clerk in the grocery store to the family members with whom we live.

Appreciation goes hand-in-hand with humility. If we are proud and think we deserve things, we don't appreciate them. "It's my right!" we say. But if we realize that we are sinners who don't have rights and don't deserve good things, then we walk humbly before God and our fellow human beings, and we appreciate whatever we receive. Humility also values others the same as we value ourselves. It makes me think, "I am no better than that alcoholic homeless person. I'll give him my other sandwich."

From a kind word to a stranger to the most intimate kindness of a spouse, our words come in many varieties. I have categorized them as cheerful and pleasant words, uplifting words, thankful words, comforting words, admonishing words, and loving words.

Cheerful and pleasant words

So many of the words we speak are neither kind nor unkind; they are simply factual, an exchange of information with others. But we are not robots; our words carry a tone. A boss who growls, "Get going, guys," doesn't generate as much of a positive atmosphere as the boss who speaks encouragingly, "Good morning, guys. Today we'll tackle the north project." He doesn't have to skip and grin all day, but a positive, friendly attitude conveys kindness.

Tone of voice and facial expression are huge factors. They express patience, tolerance, kindness, and happiness—or a lack thereof. When Mom says, "Come here, Brian," her tone can convey either irritation or cheerfulness. When I am around a person with indomitable cheerfulness, I am uplifted; I feel safe, accepted, and comfortable in his or her presence. Wouldn't it be great if we all had that effect on each other? If we wish to improve our communication skills, this is the area to begin with that will make the most impact. By simply being aware of how we sound and our impact on others, we can take steps to change. It might involve dealing with underlying issues, but that is another subject. If we shore up the self-discipline it takes to be cheerful, our emotions may just follow along.

Our positive reaction to situations and to others conveys pleasantness. Most people are in tune with the reaction of others to themselves, and they care about it. By responding to someone with calm understanding, we convey acceptance and engender a positive atmosphere. A positive atmosphere is far more likely to result in a productive relationship than a negative one is. A friend of ours grew up in an atmosphere of criticism. As an adult, many years later, he still struggles with anger, defensiveness, and low self-esteem. How do you and I react to others—especially those with whom we live or work? Let's pause, examine our initial reaction, and, if needed, replace it with a pleasant accepting one.

There may be some gender differences here. If we divide our moods into "grouchy," "neutral," or "cheerful," I assert that men operate much more in the neutral range than women. Generally speaking, they are more logical; they frequently deal with facts and information; emotions are neither here nor there. Women, however, tend more to look at life through emotions. We react positively or negatively to others and to situations. This affects our mood, making us irritable, even-tempered, or happy. I believe God meant it to be this way, minus sin, of course. Isn't this just another piece in the whole grand design of marriage between one man and one woman? Mr. Logical Smith calms down Mrs. Emotional Smith by first empathetically listening to her and then working out a solution to the problem. She in turn makes him more aware of the personal, emotional side of people so that he becomes more understanding. Together, they make a good team.

Moms have the power to set the emotional tone in the home. As the saying goes, "If Mama ain't happy; ain't nobody happy." To all mamas out there, let's use this incredible power for the good!

My cheerfulness at home, amidst the humdrum of normal life, hinges tightly with my level of humility and gratitude. When I take things for granted and walk around with "entitled" written on my attitude, I lean towards gloominess. When I count my blessings and tabulate my unworthiness, my attitude and my words are much more cheerful and pleasant.

Uplifting words

I heard a story once of a boy who was so depressed that he decided to end his life by jumping off a bridge in New York. He left a note saying that if anyone along the way would smile or speak a kind word to him, he would not go through with his plan. Nobody did. So he did.

I have always hoped this story was fictitious. I don't know, but it has spurred me on to observe people and, if the situation is appropriate, to smile or say an encouraging word like "What a pretty coat," or "You have polite children," or "Beautiful day out today, isn't it?" or "The Lord Jesus can help you." It is rare that I am rebuffed. Usually they smile in return or we have a little conversation. As a child, I remember my mom exchanging pleasant words with total strangers. Her attitude was that everybody has value, everybody is a friend, and she resolved to be especially kind to those who might be less esteemed in society. I saw the cheer she spread and have resolved to do the same.

Uplifting words are addressed to people who are sad, afraid, upset, discouraged, or lonely. Words that lift people up are comforting, protecting, understanding, and encouraging words.

On a "Focus on the Family" interview, Dee Brestin was reflecting on the loss of her husband to cancer after thirty-nine happy, yet seemingly short, years of marriage. Some of the most comforting words she heard were stories about the wonderful things Steve had done. In her sadness, she was brought closer to the happy memories of her special man.[4]

Children need lots of comforting words. When they don't understand a situation or are in pain, an embrace, a kiss, and a comment will encircle them with comfort. "Everything will be okay. Daddy will take care of you." The comfort of a parent represents the comfort of God. By instilling into our children the beautiful words of comfort found in Scripture, we teach them that the only sure place of peace is at the feet of Jesus.

When a tornado is sighted, we are told to go to the basement, get under a table, and put a pillow over our heads. Similarly, protecting words give shelter in the tornados of life. We all have our fears, some real, some imagined; children usually have more than adults. "Shelly, I will carry you when we walk past that big, barking dog." "Jason, stay right by me so you don't get lost." Our strong God tells His people dozens of times to not be afraid because He is present. "I will never leave thee, nor forsake thee" (Heb. 13:5). Romans 8:28 tells us that all things work together for good for those who love God and are called according to His purpose.

Sometimes the pain of a hurting person is exacerbated by loneliness. When he finds out someone has been in his situation and can genuinely understand, he is consoled. "I know it really hurts to have someone you love end a relationship." Even when we haven't had the same experience, we can tell them so, and try to reflect what they might be feeling. "It must be a disappointment for you not to be accepted by your favorite college." "If you need someone to talk to, I'm ready to listen anytime." The whole gospel is laced with understanding. Jesus Christ experienced every trial we could possibly go through. He leads the way and understands whatever we go through. Therefore, we can go to Him in prayer and find a faithful and understanding Friend.

To encourage is "to give courage, hope, or confidence."[5] It's like running a long-distance race. You feel you can't go on. Then your teammates shout, "You can do it! You're almost finished! Keep looking up!" Life is full of races and discouragements. A kind word of encouragement can spur us on. "Please consider counseling. Others have made their marriages work with God's almighty power." "I know you feel overwhelmed with homework, but just keep at it, one assignment at a time." "Yes, you made a mistake, but come clean and apologize. I'm sure he will forgive you." "It *is* a sad situation; let's pray to God for a solution." Encouraging words are powerful. They can inspire the downcast to reach for new plateaus. They give hope.

Thankful words

We are most thankful when we are most humble. When we

know we don't deserve a good thing, yet we still receive it, our attitude is one of gratitude. And humble, appreciative people are a joy to be with, even for themselves. I spoke once with a dean of students who dealt with foreign refugees coming to America to attend university. Freshly arrived, they were overjoyed with simple lodging, basic food, warm clothing, and bus passes. A year later, some of them requested the latest electronic equipment and a car. I am not judging them; I would do the same thing. Our standards are set to a large degree by our cultural milieu. Nonetheless, we do well to be thankful to God most of all, since He is the giver of every good and perfect gift (James 1:17), but also to family and friends. And let's not only feel it, but express it. "Thanks, honey, for working so hard today." "Thanks, sweetie, for a delicious dinner." "I appreciate it that you are working hard on that project, Devon." "Thanks for opening the door, sir." Gratitude is something that spreads cheer to both the giver and the receiver.

Admonishing words

Kind words are not always clothed in sweet pleasantness. Some we would rather not hear. But they are kind nonetheless. Genuine kindness has love and the best interest of others at heart. Some situations call for admonishment or warning; to gloss over a problem with sweet words could actually be unkind. Parenting is full of kind admonishment. "I am squeezing your hand so tightly so you don't run into the road." "If you don't eat your supper, you will eat the same food at bedtime or tomorrow morning for breakfast. I am teaching you to not be a fussy eater." "You will spend two hours doing homework after school instead of playing with your friends until your grades reflect your potential."

"Faithful are the wounds of a friend; but the kisses of an enemy are deceitful" (Prov. 27:6). Constructive criticism from a friend may hurt for a while, but after the sting subsides, we can grow and learn. Kindness is only kindness when honest and integrity are in place. Otherwise, it is flattery and deceit, like a balloon full of hot air. You thought it was big and pretty, but when it popped, there was nothing left but shriveled skin lying in the dirt. Kids cry over popped balloons; so do adults!

This wounding of a friend must always be done with gentleness and a loving heart. My husband, Joe, advocates the "sandwich principle" (see Chapter 5). Lay down the bread: "You are a great friend. I really enjoy being with you." Put the meat on the sandwich: "But there's something that bothers me. When you make a joke to a group of friends about my weaknesses, it really hurts." Another slice of bread completes the sandwich: "But I enjoy your sense of humor, and I know you don't mean to hurt me. I'm just asking you to joke about other things." And they eat the sandwich. Now some say this is political, but it's really not. Paul does it when writing to the churches, e.g., to the Philippians. This approach is also more realistic. When we criticize, we tend to think only about our complaint. By bringing in positive characteristics, we look at the big picture. It puts things into proper perspective for both people.

Loving words

All of the above types of kind words flow from varying degrees of love—love towards my neighbor in a global sense, love towards acquaintances, and love towards family and friends. But there are special loving words, often accompanied by physical affection, which we express to those who have the most special place in our hearts. A mother nuzzles her infant and says, "I love you, my darling, precious child." We tell our children, "I am so happy to see you." Romantic, intimate words, emanating from the depth of our hearts, are exchanged between couples. We have our pet names for each other. We tell our loved ones the characteristics that we love about them. We praise and compliment them. Our nonverbal demeanor complements our words. The Song of Solomon expresses deep love in a natural and a spiritual way. The words on this page cannot adequately describe the power of loving words.

My husband overflows with loving words to me and to our children. "I love you," is heard in our home many times every day. Joe is excited to see each of us when he arrives home, and he asks about the day's events. Years ago, one of our children picked up African statues of a man and a woman from the shelf, and held them as if they were kissing, and said "This is mommy and daddy." I've heard it said that one of the best things a dad can do for his children is to love their mother. By God's grace, I am blessed to be in a home filled with loving words.

It does start in the home. It's like tea being infused into hot water. Will we infuse complaints, disgust, impatience, and irritation into the teapot of our home? Or will it be flavored with kindness, warmth, safety, comfort, appreciation, and love? In writing this, I am challenged to speak more loving words. How about you? Repent before God for past sins, and lean fully on Him for wisdom for the future. Every day is new hope for a fresh start; children are amazingly optimistic, resilient, and forgiving. Let's count our blessings, and then let's tell our human blessings (our loved ones) how much we love them and why.

Conclusion

> Your talk talks,
> And your walk talks,
> But your walk talks
> More than your talk talks.

This poem graced the walls of my childhood home. It was meaningful to me because my dad doesn't talk a whole lot, but his walk speaks loudly of love. My mother talks quite a bit more, and her kind talk and her walk go together. Together, they make a great team that shows love and kindness to family and friends. Isn't that the way it should be? Let's go back to Proverbs 31:26: "In her tongue is the law of kindness." But why limit it to the homemaker? If you and I have the principle of kindness embedded in our hearts, and we resolve to let every word that exits our mouths be seasoned with kindness, wouldn't we enrich our own lives and the lives of those around us?

1. I am indebted to Dr. Flip Buys of South Africa for an unpublished paper titled "Communication," which was the source for several thoughts in the first few paragraphs of this chapter.

2. David B. Guralnik, ed. *Webster's New World Dictionary of the American Language*, Second Edition (Cleveland, Ohio: William Collins Publishers, Inc., 1980), 604.

3. Ibid., 1337.

4. Dee Brestin, interview by James Dobson, *Focus on the Family* radio broadcast, January 19, 2007.

5. David B. Guralnik, ed. *Webster's New World Dictionary of the American Language*, Second Edition (Cleveland, Ohio: William Collins Publishers, Inc., 1980), 460.

CHAPTER 12

Kindness to the Least of These

⟶•◆•⟵

The least are the most. Let's listen in. Jesus, the Master Teacher, is privately instructing His disciples on the Mount of Olives. He is telling them what will happen in the near and distant future. He said, as it were, "You will have hard times because you are a believer. Watch out for false prophets. I have given you resources. Use them wisely. Be ready at all times, because you don't know when I am coming back."

Jesus said He would return on the Day of Judgment with his angels to gather all people around Him. He would divide them into two groups. On His right will be the chosen ones who will live in heaven with Him, those who have followed Him in their lives. On His left will be those who have rejected Him and who will be cast into the torments of hell.

He describes their character as He addresses them. To those on His right, He says, "Come, ye blessed of my Father, inherit the kingdom prepared for you from the foundation of the world: for I was an hungred, and ye gave me meat: I was thirsty, and ye gave me drink: I was a stranger, and ye took me in: naked, and ye clothed me: I was sick, and ye visited me: I was in prison, and ye came unto me" (Matt. 25:34–36).

They are bewildered. They don't remember doing these things for Him. When had they seen him hungry, thirsty, homeless, naked, sick, or imprisoned?

Then comes our Lord's marvelous, humble, beautiful answer. "Verily I say unto you, Inasmuch as ye have done it unto one of the least of these my brethren, ye have done it unto me" (Matt. 25:40).

King Jesus is actually saying that the very lowliest Christian is so much a part of Himself that an act of kindness shown to one of them is the same as if it had been done to Himself. What precious, astounding love this is! He is perfectly holy, all-powerful, all-knowing, and unchangeable. And He places Himself right next to lowly sinners.

That same tender love should be so ingrained into God's children that they perform these acts without thinking about them and without expecting recognition or reward. The power of the Holy Spirit breeds compassion, love, and humility, which are the source of these acts of kindness. It then happens spontaneously, and it gives such joy that they repeat it, and it becomes a habit.

Yes, but. . .

These little acts of kindness are wonderful, we might say, but aren't they optional? What's wrong with neutrality? Isn't it enough just to live as a decent, law-abiding citizen? Let's see what Jesus says.

Jesus addresses those who did *not* feed the hungry, give a drink to the thirsty, take in strangers, clothe the naked, or visit the sick and the prisoner. His words are strong:

"Depart from me, ye cursed, into everlasting fire, prepared for the devil and his angels" (Matt. 25:41).

They are just as bewildered. They make excuses. They also ask when it was that they saw Him hungry, thirsty, homeless, naked, sick, or imprisoned. His answer is similar, yet so very different: "Inasmuch as ye did it not to one of the least of these, ye did it not to me."

Does this mean that we earn heaven with our good works? No. Jesus earned salvation for believers. "For by grace are ye saved through faith; and that not of yourselves: it is the gift of God: not of works, lest any man should boast" (Eph. 2:8–9). Rather, it is the fruit of salvation we are discussing. God's grace emanates from the believer in the form of love to the needy. It is the result of being a Christian, not the cause of it.

This passage focuses on being kind to Christians. What about the rest of the world? Galatians 6:10 clearly explains the balance: "As we have therefore opportunity, let us do good unto all men, especially unto them who are of the household of faith." Give special care to believers who are needy, then don't hold back with kindness to everyone else. And let's look for many opportunities!

The least are the most—today

What does this mean for us today? It means our worldview is turned upside-down. Rather than the rich, the famous, and the beautiful standing in our spotlight of importance, we turn our gaze to the down-and-outers.

It means we look at the man with out-of-date clothing, a crooked face, and a dripping nose, and we see gentle eyes reflecting years of devotion to God and to his family, the loss of an infant son and his wife of 55 years, and a stroke.

It means we observe a person walking with a crooked limp, speaking loudly and slowly and not very articulately, and we see a man with cerebral palsy who works full-time, who remembers everybody's name and what he told them he'd pray for that week, and who expresses heartfelt gratitude for the smallest gesture of kindness.

It means we visit the ninety-eight-year-old lady—her hair disheveled, her eyes pale and blank, her arms cradling a doll as if it were a real baby—and we see the shadow of past beauty, her long-forgotten skill for decorating and cooking, and the twinkle in her eye that is no more.

It means we watch the frazzled mother yelling at her kids in the grocery store, and we see a woman who has been abused and deserted, who is hanging on to each day by her fingernails, trying to care for her children.

Do you know some people like this? I do. Isn't it time we take them from the lower tiers of our worthiness ladder, and place them at the top, near Jesus' heart? If Jesus values His children so much that He gave His life for them, ought we not value them highly as well? God is looking at our hearts. When He sees pure motives of love and humility, He honors them. "Love God above all, and our neighbor as ourselves" is the law for life. The astounding thing is that He plants that love there in the first place, and then He rewards what reflects His own love.

Once our hearts are properly aligned, the action can start. It is amazing what small, simple deeds Jesus recognizes: a meal, a drink, clothes, a visit. Taking someone into our home is a little bigger, but we must use the opportunities we have.

God doesn't expect one person to do everything, but what opportunities has He placed on your path? Maybe you have a neighbor who is overwhelmed with her colicky newborn. Could you take care of the baby for an hour a week to give her a break? Maybe your son's friend doesn't get along with his parents and escapes to your house frequently. Could you insert bits of wisdom into dinner conversation and be an example of a loving family to him? Maybe your co-worker is facing divorce because of his violence when he's drunk. Could you answer his questions about the Bible and teach him about the Lord?

There is a large group of little people that fits the description of "the least of these." They can't speak for themselves. They can't defend themselves. They are vulnerable. They are not protected from murder by the law. They are the unborn. Too many millions have died already. Since kindness to the least of these is so important to God, then surely these little ones are at the top of the list. Let's muster all the love of our hearts and do everything in our power to defend the lives of the unborn. Even though the war against abortion has been waging for decades, let's not grow weary, but fight on for the life of these precious unborn children. It's the least we can do. Jesus said, "Suffer the little children to come unto me, and forbid them not: for of such is the kingdom of God" (Mark 10:14).

There is something very liberating about showing kindness to the least of these. We can let the floodgates of kindness go wide open. We don't have to worry about impressing others or who to be impressed by. We can simply look around us and find the most needy person, then go show love to them. No holds barred. We can allow ourselves to be vulnerable. We don't even have to worry about overdoing kindness. True kindness can't be wasted.

Jesus walked and talked kindness. He won souls by restoring broken lives. The politically correct Pharisees despised Him. The rich people didn't need Him. The strong and healthy didn't have time for Him. So He poured out His love and His Spirit to the lame, the blind, the demon-possessed, the poor, and the sinners. They repented of their sins, believed on Him, and followed Him.

For three short years, Jesus turned society on its head by making the least into the most, by taking the rejects of society and making them into Christians. His message has not dimmed. We must be Christians, and we must serve others. "And whosoever shall give to drink unto one of these little ones a cup of cold water only in the name of a disciple, verily I say unto you, he shall in no wise lose his reward" (Matt. 10:42). "Be ye kind, one to another" (Eph. 4:32).

CHAPTER 13

Your Kind of Kindness

In "Kindness Examined," we defined kindness. We analyzed our own hearts, the wellspring of kindness. We dissected the specific motives from which kindness flows. In "Kindness Learned," we discussed the development of the law of kindness in our hearts: in marriage, in parenting, and at school. We looked at kindness by children and teens. We addressed kindness gone off the tracks, seen in bullying by children. In the last section, "Kindness in Action," we described thoughts and words that are both kind and unkind. Kindness to those whom Jesus compassionately called "the least of these" was outlined. We will conclude with some practical applications of kindness and the rewards that are inherent in them.

This is the exciting part. Let's roll up our sleeves and get to work. We all have different gifts. God calls us to use the talents we have, not the ones we don't have. That's not to say that, just because I don't have the talent of sending out cards, that I shouldn't try harder to be on time with birthday cards. A little self-discipline is good for us.

There is so much that can be done. Small kindnesses are just as important as big ones. Isn't it wonderful that simply giving a cup of cold water to someone who is thirsty is highly esteemed and honored by our great God? What a motivation to do that and so much more!

En route

My favorite kind of kindness is "kindness on the way." I'm not the most efficient, plan-ahead type of person. I dream of hundreds of exhilarating acts of kindness that I never get around to, particularly sending notes of encouragement. One of these days, I'll get my act together; it'll have to be after this book is completed. But along the way, there are many possibilities.

Smiles travel the miles and bring cheer wherever they go. A kind smile acknowledges the value of someone and conveys, "Hello, fellow human being." A smile can communicate, "You're special." A smile can provide a glimmer of hope, "It'll be okay; you don't have to be sad." A smile of encouragement can say, "Hang in there, you're doing well," or "I understand; I've been there." The other day, in the grocery store, I saw an elderly man pushing the cart as his wife followed. She had a twinkle in her eye; my eyes caught hers, and she winked and smiled. She seemed to say, "I'm having fun on a grocery-shopping date with my dear husband." It was cute and it makes me cheerful every time I think back on it. Smiles are so easy to disperse, and the benefits are prolific. Let's be generous with them. (A caution to young women: be careful with your smiles, lest they be misconstrued as an invitation you don't mean to convey.)

Small courtesies take very little time or effort. Open the door for someone laden with bags or kids. Help an elderly lady lift her carry-on into the overhead bin in the airplane. Tip generously. Pick up an item someone drops and hand it to them. Say "please" and "thank you" with warmth and frequency. At social gatherings, sit with an individual or a family who is alone and strike up a conversation with them. All it takes is to be aware of the people around us, to sense their needs, and to help if we can. Of course, it's not kind to be intrusive; we have to sense our limits. If the lady on the plane has her muscle-bound son along, let him do the lifting. If it's a hundred dollar bill a lady dropped and it landed at her husband's feet, don't dive for it. Just watch to make sure they see it, and mention it to them if they don't.

Every morning, a friend of mine prays, "Lord, use me today to help or serve someone and to honor Thee." At the grocery store, she remembered her prayer as she waited and watched the wheelchair-bound lady having difficulty with her credit card. The clerk said, "I can set the food aside, and you can go home and get the cash." My friend offered, "May I swipe *my* card for you?" The woman hesitated. She continued, "Jesus Christ paid a much greater price for my sins. I'd just like to pay this bill for you." The lady smiled, "I know Him, too. Thank you very much." Both ladies went home blessed.

Serendipity and kindness: what a joy when they meet! With the law of kindness written on our hearts, we view people who share our pathway as providentially placed there. If we can show kindness in any way, it is our duty and delight to do so. Our own family members who live under the same roof come first. They are the most precious people in the world to us, though we sometimes take them for granted. "Good morning. Did you sleep well?" "How was school today?" "Can I give you a hand with that?" "Here, you can have the biggest piece." "Thanks for thinking about

me." "I love you." "Don't worry; I'll protect you at school."
Kindness is contagious; let's begin by spreading these
"germs" at home.

Everyone in the world is our neighbor, but our next-door
neighbors are conveniently close to receive our kindness: a
meal when they're sick, babysitting in a pinch, helping with
chores during difficult times, keeping a watchful eye on their
home for suspicious activity, a friendly greeting when passing by. Proverbs 27:10 reminds us that "better is a neighbor
that is near than a brother far off." Neighborhoods have the
potential for being God's breeding grounds for kindness.

When our children were toddlers, one of our neighbors
didn't like us because we had lawn care. She thought
Joe was lazy, not realizing he was working almost every
waking hour in the ministry. She thought the glow of his
computer was the glow of a TV. She refused to wave to us.
I tried to give her a pie once to sweeten our relationship,
but she gruffly refused it: "I only eat staple foods." I guess
I should've tried giving her staple foods, but I don't think
her reaction would have softened. Another neighbor, Julie,
was the complete opposite. She would be weeding, and
we would honk as we went by. She would start her wave
and her smile from the ground, before she even saw whom
she was greeting. Calvin and Esther were welcome at any
time. They loved to run over when they saw her outside.
She taught them about the plants and showed them things
around the yard. She chatted with them and gave them milk
and cookies. I felt pity for the first neighbor because I think
she had issues in her past that shaped her, but I surely have
a warm spot in my heart for dear Julie, even years later.

Cheerful words send out ripples of warmth. Some

people may think this is frivolous fluff, but I've seen people's faces light up with a little exchange of kind words. My mother has been accomplished at this for as long as I can remember. I remember her cheerful comments to the butcher, the cashier, the manager, or anyone during her trips to the grocery store when I was a child. She just seems to understand human nature. She will sense what others are thinking and express it in a positive, often humorous manner. If people respond, an interesting exchange ensues. If not, she moves on.

Acts of kindness and kind words can open the door to the greatest kindness of all, telling someone the good news of the gospel of Jesus Christ. Human love can lay the foundation for divine love to enter the heart. This is one kindness that may not be politically correct, so we may be reticent to express it. But remember the example of the travelers who came upon a roadblock that stopped them before they reached a bridge that had washed out? Their initial reaction of impatience and irritation turned to relief and gratitude when they realized that the thing that initially caused them difficulty saved their lives. Likewise, we show kindness when we warn our fellow travelers on the road to eternity that the bridge of their own righteousness has been washed out, and they will plunge into the abyss of hell unless they are saved by Jesus Christ. Prayer must precede this conversation, and love, humility, and wisdom must accompany it.

My husband has had many such conversations, especially on airplanes. Joe often asks the passengers sitting next to him about their occupation or their family, and he shares about his own life. Then he waits for an opportunity to connect the conversation to spiritual matters, possibly through beauty in nature, fulfillment in life, disappointments, or feelings of emptiness. He might share his own experiences. Then he presents the gospel in a fitting way. In order to follow up the conversation, he asks, "If I send you some free books, will you read them?" Usually, they are willing. The anonymity of air travel helps open the conversation. I believe people talk with him because he comes across with care and conviction, and because the Lord answers prayers. "Cast thy bread upon the waters" (Eccl. 11:1), and eternity will reveal the fruits of our evangelizing conversations.

The church family

The church is a community that bears each other's burdens, thereby fulfilling the law of Christ. Ministers, elders, and deacons care for the members and provide the framework of leadership, and the body of believers provides support in various ways. Organized groups within the church can do a mountain of good. I am blessed to be in a church with many active and kind members. Here are some examples of the work that is carried out. Esther Guild is a ladies' group that does charity work for our church, school, and community. Another group of men and women carries out prison ministry in several local facilities, visiting and preaching to the inmates. We have a Sunday school ministry that reaches inner-city children with singing, Bible instruction, activities, and treats. We have a mission store where we sell secondhand clothing, offer a Bible study, and provide a place to drop in for a cup of coffee, a cookie, and a chat. Our welcoming committee helps new members settle into the area. We have several missionaries we send to Africa to preach the gospel, teach seminary classes, provide day care for AIDS orphans, and offer hospice care to dying AIDS patients. Generous donors keep the wheels of these efforts going. The church can be like a motorboat, surging through the water, carrying its occupants with love, spreading waves of care and kindness into the community, and spreading the good news of the gospel of Jesus Christ.

An informal network of support in a church is a healthy sign: families socializing together, friends sharing spiritual benefits gleaned from the sermons, friendships developing, marriages germinating and flourishing, members supporting other members' businesses. Our church publishes a monthly calendar with birthdays and anniversaries on it; many kind greetings are exchanged because of it. One of our members carries out a personal ministry that I think is worth emulating. "Deb" telephones many of our older members on a regular basis. She hooks up the earpiece of her wireless phone and quietly dusts the house as she converses with lonely widows. I am sure that her cheerful nature brightens many a dull day. What creative ways can you find to express kindness to those in your church family?

Sending cards

When I think of cards, I think of many faithful, thoughtful friends who have loved and encouraged my family and me through the years. My heart fills with gratitude and my eyes fill with tears. Whether it's birthdays, anniversaries, holidays, or occasions simply to say, "thinking of you," these friends always seem to find or make the right card. It takes time and effort to do this.

These friends have varying personalities. Some are

outgoing and bubbly, and their cards are an extension of their character. Others are quiet and subdued, and their cards reflect the deep emotions that their spoken words don't express. I am a hopeless card-saver. I have a file marked "Uplifters for Joe" in which I store messages from people who have been blessed by his ministry. When he is down, I encourage him with evidence that the Lord is using his ministry for the benefit of souls. I recently culled some cards from a stack that I had saved for many years. It was like a shower of love all over again. Some of the senders had passed away, so it was a fresh reminder of friends of the past. In our age of e-mails, it is even easier to zip off a quick, kind note to someone. Cards, letters, and e-mails are a wonderful conduit for conveying kindness.

Volunteering

September 11, 2001, was a day of horror. But some good came out of this unspeakable evil. In its aftermath, President George W. Bush and others encouraged Americans to volunteer to serve others. Volunteerism has increased ever since.[1] What joy to serve meals to the homeless at a downtown mission, to play the piano at an Alzheimer's unit, to go on a mission trip and repair the homes of impoverished people, to deliver flowers to hospital patients, to donate blood, or to help build a Habitat for Humanity house. Volunteering comes naturally for some; others need to be taught. The best place to start is with children in the family setting so that serving becomes a natural part of life. Some schools are stepping up to the task and are requiring service work for graduation. Colleges and universities look at the volunteering habits of the students they consider for admission. This is a very encouraging trend. Let's hope it sets the tone for a lifestyle of volunteering.

Hospitality

"Mi casa es su casa," they said, smiling, as we entered the dirt-floor home with walls made of skids and cardboard and a roof made of scrap metal. The hostess made a sweeping motion across the dark room, and the translator indicated she indeed literally meant it, "My house is your house." We felt warmly welcomed.

Hospitality is ordained and honored by God. The Israelites of the Old Testament were instructed to love strangers in the land because they were once strangers in Egypt (Deut. 10:19). Jesus honored those who gave food, clothing, water, and a place to stay to those in need (Matt. 25:34–40). According to 1 Timothy 3:2 and Titus 1:8, the leaders of the church were chosen from among those men who were "given to hospitality." We all ought to show hospitality, in small or large ways, however God has called us, even if it requires us to go outside of our comfort zone. Our family of five once stayed several days in the home of a single, middle-aged man with cerebral palsy. He did a splendid job.

After years of receiving hospitality from others, observing my parents opening their home to guests, and having guests in our home, I have concluded several things about hospitality.

The first principle is that friendliness is foremost. If you have a simple home and serve simple food, that is fine. If you have a fancy home and serve fancy food, that is fine also. Be comfortable being yourself, and your guests will appreciate your hospitality. Relax and enjoy the experience, and they will sense your enjoyment and relax also. Your joy is contagious.

Secondly, try to anticipate the needs of your guests. If the guest bedroom is drafty, supply a space heater and extra blankets. Try to find out if your guest has dietary restrictions, and have special foods on hand to meet those needs. A cozy atmosphere is a nice extra; something as simple as flowers in a vase or a bedside lamp left on can give a warm welcome. A simple glass of water or juice at just the right time is a kind gesture.

Finally, aim to please. If someone stays with you a few days, find out their needs and intentions, then work out a schedule. If you can't take them somewhere, arrange for someone who can. Invite them to help themselves to snacks and drinks. Don't forget to serve your own family; most guests don't want your children to be left out. If your guests sincerely wish to help with the dishes, let them, and enjoy more fellowship while you work. If they'd rather sit in the living room with a cup of coffee, do the dishes later. Try to balance the conversation between showing interest in the guests and sharing your own thoughts. If you can say, "Your pleasure is my pleasure," you are on your way to some rewarding experiences.

"Let brotherly love continue. Be not forgetful to en- tertain strangers: for thereby some have entertained angels unawares" (Heb. 13:1–2).

Generosity

Kindness and generosity go hand-in-hand. The biblical principle is to give wisely with a loving heart. "And though

I bestow all my goods to feed the poor, and though I give my body to be burned, and have not charity [steadfast love], it profiteth me nothing" (1 Cor. 13:3). John said generosity is a mark of grace in the life of the believer. "But whoso hath this world's goods, and seeth his brother have need, and shutteth up his bowels of compassion from him, how dwelleth the love of God in him? My little children, let us not love in word, neither in tongue; but in deed and in truth" (1 John 3:17–18).

Jesus honored the poor widow for giving her mite (one-eighth of a cent) more than he honored the rich people who gave much more. Why? Because she gave all she had, and they gave their extra. God knows our hearts. He instructs us to give. "The Lord loveth a cheerful giver" (2 Cor. 9:7). Generosity is part of loving God above all and our neighbor as ourselves.

Kind generosity is not to be confused with enabling irresponsible behavior. Indiscriminately giving money to those whose bad habits have gotten them into a financial bind would enable them to continue sinning. We can help them in other ways, like paying for counseling or rehabilitation.

With obedience comes blessing. God openly offers rewards for generosity: "He that hath pity upon the poor lendeth unto the Lord; and that which he hath given will he pay him again" (Prov. 19:17). What might start out with less-than-pure motives may change. God will patiently teach us. He may encourage us with spiritual rewards and material rewards. "He that hath mercy on the poor, happy is he" (Prov. 14:21b). If we show we can handle His gifts for His glory, he might give us responsibility for wealth. A philanthropic friend of ours says, "You can't out-give the Lord. He keeps replacing what I give." Our generous God has assigned us to be stewards over the money He has given us.

Doesn't this give soaring freedom? The money's not ours; it belongs to the Lord. We simply have to ascertain how much we need to live, whether the cause to be donated to is in God's favor, and give! Then we can just wait for the blessings and for the next opportunity to be generously kind. Do be forewarned, though: it's addictive!

In the workplace

Meanness is out; kindness is in. This is the observation of columnist Marilyn Gardner.[2] A number of books promote and document an increase of kindness in the workplace. Business leaders are realizing that a philosophy of kindness flowing through the company results in improved customer relations, more dedicated employees, increased productivity, and lower turnover. Customers and employees naturally respond positively when treated with dignity and respect.

Other factors are inherent in kindness, such as honesty and openness. If two parties make an agreement that sounds favorable to both and their negotiations are congenial, but one party realizes later that the fine print was not what he was lead to believe, that is not kindness.

Fairness is also an ingredient of kindness. When the CEO of a floundering company receives an exorbitant salary for cutting and slashing jobs, it may be downsizing, but their extreme wealth comes at the expense of the misery and misfortune of others. If we offer a ridiculously low price for a piece of property to a seller who is going bankrupt because of health problems, it may be how the market operates, but it is not kind. God forbad the Israelites from earning interest from the poor (Ex. 22:25), but some of our contemporary practices go way beyond that.

The kind and honest company still must make a profit to survive. This is the balance that companies must work hard to achieve in a highly competitive, capitalistic world. It is a challenging task. They must be skilled and knowledgeable, yet considerate. Kindness doesn't mean giving the store away. Kindness doesn't mean allowing yourself to be taken advantage of. Many companies have successfully achieved this balance, but many have fallen as well.

It really boils down to each of us doing our part to show kindness to whomever we meet. It's exciting to think of the opportunities and the transformation that could take place in the workplaces of this world if we are all kind.

In-depth kindness

A number of people who work in our church's Sunday School ministry have dedicated their time, resources, and hearts to some inner-city families. In order to bring the loving gospel of Jesus Christ to these needy sinners, they build relationships by bringing the children to Sunday School, taking them on outings, getting involved in their families, sharing their personal lives with them, enjoying each other's company, praying for them, and simply being friends.

I have heard stories of drug addicts who have been mentored—you might say hounded—by Christians over a period of years. In the end, the perseverance of their friends through the power of the Holy Spirit finally won over their hearts, so that they now live godly, productive lives.

These mentors are to be greatly admired. This is not just kindness on the way; it requires self-sacrifice and long-term dedication. At times it demands giving up personal time in order to do unpleasant tasks. The rewards often come in the form of "three steps forward, two steps back," if they come at all. It's a battle against innate sin, dysfunctional home training, the power of addiction, a lack of initiative, the evil forces of our culture, or any combination of these influences. It's a battle against Satan himself.

So what is the motivation of these mentors? It's Spirit-worked love for God and for people. It's the Golden Rule written upon the heart. It's caring so much for the well-being of another that their pain and joy become ours.

I challenge you to pray for the opportunity to impact someone's life for the good. Who has God placed in your pathway? Maybe there is someone there right now who you need to notice: maybe a boy with an absentee father, or an unwed mother, or a lonely foreign family, or someone addicted to porn or alcohol. Let's examine ourselves. Are we willing to make the sacrifice? Are we willing to invite someone into our comfortable circle in order to share family love? Let's start small and build, asking for God's guidance along the way, and see what the Lord will do with us for the benefit of another soul and our own. And let's experience this joy that is both the driving force and the fruit of in-depth kindness.

A blanket of kindness

"The effectual fervent prayer of a righteous man availeth much" (James 5:16). We each need to pray for God's blessing on our own efforts of kindness, but it is also one of the greatest kindnesses to pray for blessings for other people; in fact, it is essential for each of us to do. Praying for the benefit of others is like putting a warm blanket on a cold person. Our Father in heaven promises us good things if we ask for them in His Name (Matt. 7:11; John 14:13). This can be done during our daily devotions or when someone comes to mind during the course of the day. It can be long or short.

When my husband visits elderly people who complain that they aren't able to help others very much anymore, he urges them to use their many hours confined to home for intercessory prayer. First, they ought to pray for their own family, then for their church family, then for the human family at large. God often lays a burden on the heart of individual Christians to pray for a particular person or issue or endeavor. My mother-in-law has always prayed faithfully; I really believe the Lord has answered many of those prayers, as seen in the lives of a number of her descendants converted and now working diligently in the kingdom of Jesus Christ. John Bunyan said that you can do more than pray after you've prayed, but you cannot do more than pray until you have prayed.

Life-consuming kindness

Millions on this globe dedicate their entire lives to disseminating mercy. Men and women in healthcare work many hours to alleviate pain and suffering and to find cures for diseases. Mission workers often sacrifice their own comfort to bring peace and comfort to the poor and needy in modern cities and in developing countries. Peace Corps volunteers use their training and talents in 139 different countries to work on issues ranging from AIDS relief to business development.³ Those in the armed forces willingly put themselves in harm's way, or support those who do, for the sake of freedom and peace. Ministers and ministry workers expend their energy daily to serve souls in churches and in charitable organizations. Parents adopt children, some of whom are handicapped or have been neglected or abused. Counselors, foster parents, and others in the field of social work fulfill a plethora of needs. Law enforcement officers carry out their potentially dangerous job with tenderness to the weak and justice to criminals. And there are so many more.

It's awe-inspiring to think about this multitude that serves, especially those who do so with selflessness. The gratitude is often not commensurate with the sacrifice. If you are one of them, I commend you and thank you and encourage you to persevere. The rewards will find you, if they haven't already.

Walking in the footsteps of Jesus

Aside from what Jesus Himself endured, none return kindness for cruelty more than persecuted Christians. "Aban," from Bangladesh, has been a Christian in this increasingly Muslim country for twenty years. Although he communicates poorly, he has evangelized many. He diligently helps people, digging ditches and assisting whenever he can, without being asked.⁴ Yet he was shunned by his family. His wife, "Momina," was beaten by her family. She was thrown out of her home under threat of being poisoned for turning away from the Muslim faith to Christianity. Even though this family has been chased from twenty-two villages over the years, they continue to bring the gospel of the Lord Jesus Christ and to show courageous love to their persecutors. Aban and Momina, and millions in countries like Vietnam, Sudan, China, Indonesia, and North Korea, live close to their Savior, sharing His Word and showing His love. When they suffer and when some are martyred, they are happy to be even closer to Him.[5]

Kindness no matter what

Kindness is beautiful—not only to receive, but especially to give. Is the law of kindness written on your heart? Do you practice kindness no matter what? Remember the parable of the Good Samaritan, that wonderful story of the underrated foreigner helping the nearly dead robbery victim? Jesus concluded with these words, "Go and do thou likewise."

---

1. "Volunteerism rates near historic high," *Grand Rapids Press*, April 16, 2007, A3.

2. "At Work, 'Nice' Is on the Rise," *Christian Science Monitor*, October 17, 2006.

3. The Peace Corps, "What is the Peace Corps?" The Peace Corps, http://www.peacecorps.gov/index.cfm?shell=learn.whatispc

4. Tom White, "The Man Who Mumbled," *Voice of the Martyrs*, August, 2007, 2.

5. Dory Puffe and Charlie Banks, "Bangladesh, 'God Makes Us Brave,'" *Voice of the Martyrs*, August, 2007, 3–5.

APPENDIX

"Mommy, please don't go!"

What is your career? I have several. They are: chef, gardener, sanitation expert, manager, secretary, nurse, teacher, chauffeur, counselor, arbitrator, company vice-president, security guard, interpreter, salesperson, purchaser, interior decorator, receptionist, waitress, financial advisor, and back-up maintenance lady. I have had formal training for some of my careers; most I have learned by experience. I am on duty twenty-four hours a day, seven days a week. The pay isn't fantastic, but the rewards are unbeatable! During the first few years of my simultaneous careers, my scope is very narrow, but with every passing year, the impact of my investment of time and energy increases exponentially, even into eternity. I do have moments of boredom, but then I think of the long-term effects of my work. I realize that even the great pyramids of Egypt were built one stone at a time. I never have to wonder what my purpose in life is. I am wanted and needed and loved by my subordinates. I have moments of great frustration and moments of great fulfillment. I assert that I have far more fulfillment than anyone with just one career. I have many short- and long-term goals that I am constantly adjusting and accomplishing. My career begins at the top of the corporate ladder, and it stays there until the end of my life. The name of my corporation is *My Family*. I am a mother.

The subject of mothers having a career or staying at home is a sensitive one. There are women on both sides of the issue, and many caught between, who have passionate feelings on the issue, and who love their children. I will try to treat this subject in a compassionate tone. At the same time, I would like to make the case that it is the healthiest, most natural, kindest, and most scriptural approach to childrearing for a mom to be with her children as much as possible.

First, though, a word to single moms and those who simply must work to make ends meet. You struggle with carrying the load of a job and caring for a household. You long to be home more with your children, but you simply can't be. My friend, my prayers are with you. Cast all your cares upon the Lord; He will care for you (1 Pet. 5:7). He promises He will. Just follow in God's ways and trust Him with the results. God doesn't promise an easy life to His followers, but He does promise a blessed life. I wonder if God might place single moms in the same special group in which He places widows. If that's the case, then you are the focus of His care (Ps. 146:9). The following persuasions for moms to be home are not meant to increase your anxiety or guilt.

Your career

You have gone to school a number of years. You are in a position that has many opportunities, which in turn increase with your level of commitment. You enjoy the challenge, the stimulation, and the benefits. Yet you hear the clock ticking—the biological clock, that is. You listen. You have your baby. Six weeks of maternity leave is barely enough to get your strength back and return the household into some sense of normalcy. You go back to work, and your baby goes off to day care. You see your baby a few hours in the evening, before you drop into bed exhausted, only to get up at 6:00 a.m. to do it all over again. You need some relaxation on the weekend, so baby has a babysitter and you and your husband go out to dinner. Baby grows up. Your toddler calls the babysitter "Mama." The babysitter witnesses your child's first step. At first, your toddler begs you not to leave her, but later she doesn't seem to mind when you go. You feel frazzled from trying to fulfill the duties of a full-time job while maintaining the household, but you are caught up in the whirl and don't know how to stop the cycle.

I am afraid this scene is replayed in thousands of households in our contemporary society. It is the norm for mothers of young children to work outside the home. It has gone so far that stay-at-home moms feel they must qualify their occupation with an apology: "I am *just* a housewife."

You can stay home!

But there is hope on the horizon! The tide is coming back in. Career women are feeling the empty spot in their hearts that longs to be filled with children. They are realizing their career isn't as full as they had hoped, and mothering isn't as empty as it once seemed. And, thank the Lord, more are staying at home to be with their children. I would like to set before you reasons for moms to stay at home as much as possible; then I will offer encouragement and suggestions for carrying it out.

It makes sense

There is a *good* reason for staying home. If we, as mothers, listen to the inner voice of our hearts, most of us hear the call to care for our children. We want to feed them, protect them, and train them. Those who work outside the home also go through great pains to provide care for their children; it is just carried out by someone else. I believe it is ordained by God that the child I carried in my womb for nine months is such an intimate part of me that I am best suited to be that child's primary caregiver. Who can love my child better than I can? Who can best care for and protect him? It really is the most sensible way.

Bonding

There is a *better* reason. A mother at home is better for the child. There is a plethora of research that has been done on mother-child bonding. Much of it is conflicting, but there is consistency. Children who are sent to some form of day care, especially under the age of one, are more likely to have anxiety or insecurity in the area of attachment or bonding.[1] The child himself manifests this every time he cries out, "Mommy, please don't go!" When children are assured Mommy is consistently present, they don't have to worry about missing her, and they can get on with childhood. As children grow into preteen and teen years, the mother in the home provides stability, accessibility, and reassurance. Mom does need breaks, and it is healthy for a child to interact with others, but it is important for children to know Mom is their safety net. I read once that a baby falls in love with its mother around six months of age. Typical maternity leaves don't allow time for this to happen.

Most infants are tenaciously committed to their mothers. This is apparent at an early age. The newborn burrows into the warmth of his mother's arms at feeding time. He reaches out for mom in times of anxiety. He expresses verbally and nonverbally that he needs her and wants her. She is there to nurture him and train him. The commitment goes both ways, and it continues unless something interferes. The nature of the commitment changes with age, always moving toward independency. But mother-child commitment is one of the central beams upon which the house of our personality is built.

The consistency of a mother staying at home prevents a child from falling through the cracks. Bad habits and naughty behavior can be nipped in the bud. One caregiver offers more consistency than multiple ones can. A mother can offer focused instruction and discipline from infancy to adulthood according to biblical teachings. A consistent schedule, the proper amount of sleep, time to play, time to learn how to do age-appropriate tasks, and an absence of the stress that comes with being shuttled around are more advantages of having a mother at home. Both quality time and quantity time are needed.

Home is a place of refuge. Each of us mothers wants to be the best mother she can be. Our children express their need and love for us. Kindness is answering that call for love with, "Yes, I am here for you now, and I'll be here in the future."

Scripture

Then there is the *best* reason. It is the way of Scripture. Proverbs 31 describes the virtuous woman. She is pictured in the role of wife first—she takes very good care of her husband. Then the author details how she cares for the household, including the children. She makes clothing, purchases food, buys land, does physical work, sells her quality merchandise, rises before dawn, and works after dusk. She does charity work, speaks with wisdom and kindness, is diligent, and follows God. Her reward is that her children call her blessed, and her husband and others praise her. We all have our strengths and weaknesses, but the bottom line is that we must spend our time caring for our husband and children, and we must love and fear the Lord. In Titus 2:4–5, Paul instructs older women to "teach younger women to be sober, to love their husbands, to love their children, to be discreet, chaste, *keepers at home*, good, obedient to their own husbands, that the word of God be not blasphemed" (emphasis added). As Elizabeth Elliot wonders, "When we have set for ourselves so ambitious an agenda [of having a career], is there time to do those things that are clearly the will of God?"[2]

Options

I hope you are convinced that being a stay-at-home mom is the best approach to mothering. I think the world would be a more stable and safe place if all moms were home when their children were home. It is an ideal for which we should all pray. Yet I must be realistic and examine some options.

Part-time

Moms, some of you are partially convinced. You might say, "We simply can't make it on my husband's income alone, even if we downsize." Or, "I need to keep my foot in the door in my line of work." Or, "I would go crazy being at home all day!" Some women can work part-time; being at home part of the time is better than being absent from your children all day, every day. And maybe Dad, rather than a babysitter, can be with the children. Is it possible for you to take a five- to ten-year sabbatical from your career and return when your youngest child enters school? Then you will have been there for those important formative years. Can you run a business out of your home? Is homeschooling an option? For those with children in school, can you find a position that allows you to get your children off to school in the morning and be there when they arrive home? Many teens get into trouble with the law during after-school hours. Be creative in finding a solution.

In the event that we do need others to care for our children, it is important to find the best possible caregiver to take our place. Children are resilient, but they can be damaged emotionally, spiritually, and physically. They are irreplaceable. Please be sure to check out thoroughly the environment you are placing your child in to make sure it matches your biblical principles. I would pick relatives first, providing they share your Christian beliefs. My second choice would be a babysitter in a home setting, and my last choice, day care.

There is a price
Whatever decision you make, expect sacrifices to be necessary. It is inherent in parenting to make sacrifices. If you aren't willing to give up many of your own desires for the welfare of your child, then please don't bring a child into this world. Don't burden yourself, your child, or others by

having a baby just "because that's what every other couple does." You will need to ask yourself some serious questions and make some life-changing decisions. And once you have entered the stream of childrearing, there is no exiting. But there are excellent tools available for keeping afloat.

If you have that child already, then you know the meaning of sacrifice. If you are bucking against it, it would be in your best interest (and your child's) to give up the battle, roll up your sleeves, and set about the task of childrearing in a scriptural manner. But you don't have to do it alone; God is able and willing to help. Just ask Him.

There are rewards

Here is the good news! After you have made the decision and commitment to sacrifice, I can assure you the rewards far exceed the sacrifice. "The father of the righteous shall greatly rejoice: and he that begetteth a wise child shall have joy of him. Thy father and thy mother shall be glad, and she that bare thee shall rejoice" (Prov. 23:24–25; see also Ps. 127:3–5, Prov. 17:6). Usually, the greater your investment, the greater your rewards. Childrearing is the culmination of a million experiences resulting in a full-grown, mature, contributing member of society. You are in the midst of childrearing; why not give it your all? Whatever you sow, you will reap.

Suggestions and Encouragement

Many others have traveled this road before and left a paper trail—in the form of information and books.[3] I offer here several condensed suggestions and encouragements.

Money

You may believe a mother should stay at home, but, for many of you, the bottom line is money. Downsizing and simplifying may be the answer for you: buying a smaller house and older cars, shopping at thrift shops and garage sales, living on a budget, using coupons, eating out less, and giving up services like lawn care. It may be painful, but let me encourage you with a quote from one who successfully accomplished this.

> *I believe in the sovereignty of our Lord. I believe he can orchestrate events to create a level of provision that astounds us.*
>
> *I believe that there are times when he requires us to step out in faith even though we feel doomed. Sometimes, to grow in faith, we must jump and learn he will catch us. I have seen it in my own life. I would have never attempted being a stay-at-home mom if I'd simply looked at the impossible economic equation. I had to step out in faith. In my life, in countless others throughout time, God has blasted through the boundaries of common sense and logic to put land under the feet and food on the table of his people. For my family.[4]*

It may require some of you to take a step down on the economic ladder, but it is worth the price. Look at it as a challenge and enjoy it. It won't be easy, but God is there to help when we pray. If you begin to falter, make a list of the items you have to do without, then compare it with a picture in your mind of your son or daughter, grown up and molded in the way God promises, and ask yourself which one you would rather have.

A well-rounded home

The first thing you might notice as you change from being a career woman to a stay-at-home mom is an absence of the sense of frenzied panic. You might not go so far as to call it "tranquility," but when you can focus on your children, your home, and your husband, you can make your home a haven of rest. Being diligent without being frantic will bring more peace of mind.

Did someone say "husband"? Where has he been all this time? That is the next thing you will notice. You now have time to pay more attention to him. By making your home a haven of rest, you bolster your marriage. How about fixing his favorite meal or restoring order in the house, post career-tornado? Remember, as his wife, it is your privilege to show him respect and to serve him with Christian love. Don't be surprised if he begins to love and serve you more as well. But don't worry about that for now; just do your part.

Here is a precaution regarding husbands. There is a tendency in some families for the wife to become so wrapped up in the children that she ignores her husband and takes over the home domain. He feels increasingly excluded as the leader God meant him to be and becomes more involved in work. His circle is work, hers is home, and ne'er do the two intersect. A breeding ground is laid for marital distance, tension, and even an affair. Don't let this creep up on you. Women, keep yourself attractive, stimulate yourself with knowledge in your husband's field, have daily conversations about your experiences without whining, don't let grudges fester, compliment and thank each other, go out on dates regularly, keep in touch with each other's feelings and your own, and keep being affectionate.

Attitude determines latitude

Our attitude is tremendously important. We can either see our home as solitary confinement or as an adventure base from which to explore the world with our children. Our attitude will affect our level of happiness, and nothing spills over to everyone else like mom's mood! Our tone of voice is as pervasive as the weather: the sun shines and the shadows flee, or the dreariness, cold, and rain chill us to the bone. As we carry out chores that seem like drudgery, why not sing? The result is that our children learn songs and feel the cheerful environment. Here is a chance to talk and teach along the way (Deut. 6:7–9). When our children are naughty, we can use these very important moments to teach them positive character traits such as generosity, honesty, and kindness. By involving them in the daily running of the household, we bond and they learn. The opportunities are endless, and that is a very exciting thought indeed! Why not be positive?

"It's just not that easy!" I know these precise struggles: headaches, hormones, fatigue, boredom, irritations, and discouragements. My experience is that spending time with the Lord, confessing my sins and weaknesses, thanking Him for His blessings, adoring Him, and asking for His help throughout the day bring the best help I could ever find. My most frequent prayer as I go through the day is "Lord, help me." And remember, "All things work together for good to them that love God, to them who are the called according to his purpose" (Rom. 8:28). God is in charge. He knows what He is doing. Rest in His wisdom.

Missing out

Most of us don't want to miss out on excitement. We won't have to worry about that if we are home. We get the exclusive privilege of witnessing important milestones in our child's life: the first step, the first laugh, and those precious comments from a child's point of view. Don't you want to be the recipient of that unmitigated devotion, rather than the babysitter? It's the foundation upon which your lifetime relationship with your child is built. A young man once told me, "Ever since I was a baby, my mother had other people take care of me. I was carted around everywhere. I really don't feel devoted to her. She wasn't there for me; I don't feel like being there for her." Working moms are devoted to their children, but when someone else is physically present most of their waking hours, children don't always realize how much their mother loves them. Direct love beats second-party love.

You might be worried you will lose a sense of fulfillment. I challenge you that if you look for it, you will find it. But if you only slog through each day, you won't find fulfillment. Challenge yourself to be the best mom you can be. Set your ideals high. Write them down; check them periodically. Read good books. Keep your mind stimulated. See the potential in your child and tap into your child's strengths and challenge him or her to be an excellent plumber, doctor, therapist, or mother!

Look for ways to involve your children in a variety of activities that fulfill multiple goals. For example, visit a nursing home. Converse with the elderly people about their experiences, bring them a child-made gift, or sing to them.

You'll bring great joy to them, and your children will see the spectrum of life, valuing those who have lived a full life.

The frustration factor

Let's face the facts. Childrearing is fraught with frustration. First and foremost, pray ahead of time to prevent a crisis. Then pray during and after a crisis. Seek advice in Scripture, good books, and from wise family and friends. Learn from your mistakes and move on. Take your sins to Christ for forgiveness. Don't keep punishing yourself. Be in touch with your feelings, both positive and negative, so that you understand your own emotions and how they affect you. For instance, if you know the pre-dinner time is very frustrating, try to do some food preparation earlier in the day.

Deal with anger properly. Take care of yourself physically with proper nutrition and exercise. And take some time for yourself away from the kids. *"She's Gonna Blow!"* by Julie Ann Barnhill takes an honest, sometimes light-hearted look at motherly frustration.[5] On a more serious note, child abuse is a real danger that we ought not dismiss as something we would never do. Children do have the potential for driving us to despair. We can't let ourselves get so bottled up that we explode at the people we love the most. It is kindest to be a stay-at-home mom, but if our kindheartedness has taken wings, it's time to pamper ourselves and take a break. We must take care of ourselves spiritually and emotionally in order to keep giving of ourselves to our family.

The greatest incentive

You can't take material goods with you to eternity. But here is good news: your most valuable assets, your children, can go with you! Out of His stupendously loving heart, God the Father gave up *His one and only Son* to live among sinners in a sinless way, to die on the cross, and to live again so that sinners like you and your children can live with Him in heaven forever. God's covenant is one of His greatest gifts. He actually promises He will work through families, by the power of His Spirit, saving people down through the generations. Don't you want to do everything in your power to lead your children on that pathway that leads to God Himself? We are nurturing eternal souls.[6] Nothing else is more important.

---

1. Robert Karen, *Becoming Attached* (Oxford: Oxford University Press, 1994), 318.

2. "A Woman's Mandate," *Family Practice*, ed. R.C. Sproul, Jr. (Phillipsburg, N.J.: P&R Publishing Co., 2001), 59.

3. Valuable resources are listed in other footnotes. Others are: Cheri Fuller, *The Mom You're Meant to Be* (Wheaton, Ill.: Tyndale House Publishers, Inc., 2003). Cheryl Gochnauer, *Stay-at-Home Handbook* (Downers Grove, Ill.: Intervarsity Press, 2002).

4. Allie Pleiter, *Becoming a Chief Home Officer* (Grand Rapids: Zondervan, 2002), 161.

5. Julie Ann Barnhill, *She's Gonna Blow!* (Eugene, Ore.: Harvest House, 2001).

6. Dee Brestin, interview by James Dobson, *Focus on the Family* radio broadcast, February 4, 2005.

Study Questions

Chapter 1: What is Kindness?

1. List one experience of kindness and one of unkindness that you have had or observed.

2. What is kindness? Write a summary statement.

3. Look up Matthew 22:40 and Ephesians 4:32. How important is kindness to God? Give two reasons.

4. Read Luke 10:25–37. Analyze the parable of the Good Samaritan. Which behaviors fit the definition of "kindness" and "unkindness"? Why? Explain what thoughts were behind each action. What was Jesus trying to teach here?

5. How important is kindness to you? What emotions do you experience when someone is kind to you? Unkind? What is your behavior in response to kindness? To unkindness?

6. What is one new way you can show a small kindness to someone in your life? A large kindness?

Chapter 2: The Roots of Kindness

1. Share an experience in which you have been the recipient of an act of pure kindness.

2. In your own words, describe the difference between kindness done out of saving grace and kindness done out of common grace.

3. Read Galatians 5:22–23. List each component of the fruit of the Spirit. How is each one related to kindness?

4. Examine Galatians 6:1–10. What does "the law of Christ" mean (v. 2)? What is involved in fulfilling this law?

5. How "good" and kind can an unbeliever be? How bad and unkind can a believer be? What do you think God thinks of a well-behaved unbeliever and a poorly behaved believer? How do you think other people react to them?

6. What are two ways you can show kindness to others so that it fits the description of being a "good work"?

Chapter 3: Our Motives

1. Pick one motive for kindness listed in this chapter. Tell a story that fits the description of that motive.

2. Other motives are often mixed in with kind motives. Name a few.

3. Second Peter 1:5–11 describes how a Christian progresses in spiritual maturity. What happens to our motives for kind behavior as we become more mature?

4. Read the stories of Pharaoh's daughter (Ex. 2:6–10), Rahab (Josh. 2:6–16), and Ruth (Ruth 1:14–18 and 2:2–12). What motive did each of these women have for carrying out acts of kindness? Explain your answer.

5. What makes Christ's kindness the greatest of all?

6. Describe two ways in which you could challenge yourself to show kindness out of selfless motives.

Chapter 4: The Kind Wife

1. In your mind, what is a kind wife like?

2. Look at Genesis 2:20–3:24. If we compare the wife's role in the Garden of Eden, before sin entered the world, to her role after the fall, what are some similarities? What are some differences?

3. Consider Ephesians 4:31–5:2. What happens when anger and an unforgiving spirit stir inside a wife? How are kindness and forgiveness connected? When love is alive in a marriage, what kinds of kindnesses happen?

4. Why is it kind for a wife to respect her husband? Read Ephesians 5:22–33. What are the benefits when a wife is more concerned with fulfilling her own duties than with correcting her husband? What are the benefits when a wife understands the thoughts and feelings of her husband?

5. When a wife compliments her husband, how does he benefit? How does she benefit?

6. Our society looks askance at the principle of a sub-missive wife. What are two defenses for this biblical concept?

7. If you are a wife, what are two areas in your marriage where you are inspired to practice the law of kindness to your husband in new ways? Consider the obstacles and make a plan to reach your goal.

Chapter 5: The Kind Husband

1. In your mind, what is a kind husband like?

2. In God's design for the family, He placed the husband as head of his wife. What does this mean? What does this *not* mean? Consider Ephesians 5:22–33.

3. Jesus Christ is the model for husbands to follow. Name two specific ways a husband should follow Christ's example. See Ephesians 5:22–33 again.

4. Study Colossians 3:12–14 and 1 Peter 3:7. Choose two of these virtues and describe how the kind husband can put each one into practice in his marriage.

5. When a husband compliments his wife, how does she benefit? How does he benefit?

6. What are the benefits when a husband understands the thoughts and feelings of his wife? Should he work with her emotions, against them, or some of each? The husband's greatest need is to be respected; the wife's greatest need is to be loved. How can the kind husband show love?

7. If you are a husband, what are two areas in your marriage where you are challenged to practice the law of kindness to your wife in new ways? Consider the obstacles and make a plan to reach your goal.

Chapter 6: Parenting with Kindness

1. In your mind, what is a kind parent like?

2. Why is it important for parents to have a consistent, biblical philosophy of kindness?

3. Isaiah 49:14–16 and 66:13 compare the love of a mother with the love of God. Name three ways they are similar.

4. Read Luke 15:11–32. The father of the prodigal had a heart of love for his son. How did he show this love? The father's love is an example of Christ's love. How can the kind parent show love during a child's rebellion?

5. Discipline may not seem kind to children. Name two examples in which a parent's action does not seem kind in the eyes of children, but it really is. Be specific.

6. If you are a parent, what are two areas where you would like to improve in relation to kindness? Design a plan of action for these goals.

Chapter 7: The Teacher's Role

1. In your mind, what is a kind teacher like?

2. How important is it for a teacher to teach and model kindness? Give reasons for your answer.

3. Jesus Christ was a master teacher who used parables to explain lessons. Read Luke 13:6–10 and 15:3–7. What principles was He teaching in these parables? How do they apply to teaching today?

4. Proverbs 6:16–19 lists the seven things that God hates. List one positive action a teacher can do to prevent each of these evil things from happening.

5. How much does a child's training at home influence how kind he is? If a child has poor training at home, how much can a teacher do to counteract unkindness?

6. If you are a teacher, name two methods you can implement in order to promote kindness or prevent unkindness among your students. If you are not a teacher, write down two ideas on this topic.

Chapter 8: Bullying

1. Have you ever had an experience with bullying, whether as a bully, a victim, or an observer? Would you feel free to share it?

2. What is the difference between teasing and bullying?

3. What help does God offer to the victim of bullying? See Psalm 50:15, Matthew 5:11–12, and Matthew 7:7–11. What good can come out of this traumatic experience?

4. Cain bullied Abel. What were Cain's thoughts in this situation which led to such a tragic ending? Can you describe a similar modern-day situation, either a real or a hypothetical one?

5. How serious is bullying? Is it a normal activity of childhood? Should we let it run its course or should we fight it?

6. If you know of a bullying situation, what can you do to counteract it? If you were to counsel a bully, a victim, or an observer, what would you say to each of them?

Chapter 9: A Letter to Children and Teens

1. Have you ever had an experience with bullying, as either a bully, a victim, or a bystander? Would you feel free to share it?

2. In the story, "Robert's Revenge," Robert's attitude towards Peter changed drastically. What was his attitude before? After? What was it that changed him?

3. We all want to be happy. Read the last section of this chapter, "All of us." What is the one thing that all of us need? How do we search for it?

4. Read the story of Joseph in Genesis 37, 39, and 40. Describe two ways in which he was bullied. How did he react?

5. What ideas do you have for stopping bullying at school? At home? In your neighborhood?

6. a. If you are a victim of bullying, what are some actions you could possibly take to improve your situation?

b. If you are a bully, take a moment alone or with a mentor, and write down the reasons you do unkind things to others, and how you feel when you do this, as well as how the other person probably feels. Write out a plan for changing your behavior.

c. If you are a bystander who sees bullying, what action could you take to improve the situation?

Chapter 10: Kind Thoughts

1. Relate a story about when you misunderstood circumstances, made a wrong conclusion, and later found out the real situation.

2. Name two of the "signposts for kind thoughts." Define them in your own words and give an example for each.

3. Read 1 Corinthians 13. What is the overarching principle that must rule our thoughts? What is one way that thoughts can affect our actions according to this principle?

4. Read Romans 15:5 and 1 Peter 3:8. What is Scripture's wisdom on how believers are to think about and feel towards each other?

5. What are two ways that we can deter ourselves from assessing a situation inaccurately?

6. Think about your thoughts. What are two areas in which you can challenge yourself to kinder thoughts and attitudes?

Chapter 11: Kind Words

1. Give one example of kind words and one example of unkind words that were spoken to you. How did you feel?

2. Of the types of unkind words discussed in this chapter, which do you believe is the most damaging? Why? Of the types of kind words listed, which is the most uplifting? Why?

3. Words reveal what is in the heart. List four ways in which the words of a foolish person differ from those of a wise person. Consult Proverbs 14 and 15.

4. Do you agree with James 3:2, 6, and 8? What damage can these words do? How can we counteract these evil words in ourselves? In others?

5. Read Proverbs 15:23 and 25:11. According to Scripture, how important is a fitting word spoken at a good time? Give an example.

6. In what new situations and to whom would you like to speak kindly? Write up a plan to achieve this goal.

Chapter 12: Kindness to the Least of These

1. Describe the characteristics of some people you know who might fit the description of "one of the least of these" in Matthew 25:40.

2. Compare the two groups of people in Matthew 25:33–46. How were their behaviors different? How were their hearts different? How did the King treat them differently?

3. Read Psalm 112:9, Proverbs 14:21, Acts 20:35, and Romans 15:1–6. What are the rewards that come to those who show kindness to the least of these?

4. Jesus is King; yet He reached out to the underprivileged, the sick, and the poor. What in God's character moved Him to do this? Consult Isaiah 40:11, Matthew 11:29, and Philippians 2:1–8.

5. How is this compassionate attitude of Jesus different from the attitude we observe in our culture and in our own natural hearts?

6. Look around you. Do you see "one of the least of these my brethren"? What can you do to help that fits with Matthew 25:40? Challenge yourself to go beyond your comfort zone.

Chapter 13: Your Kind of Kindness

1. What is your favorite kind of kindness to give? To receive?

2. Choose one of the categories from this chapter, and describe an experience that relates to it.

3. Kindness is not just words and deeds. What qualities are found in the heart that give rise to kindness? Consult 1 Corinthians 13, 2 Corinthians 9:6–8, and Ephesians 4:32.

4. Compare Nehemiah 5:1–13 with Luke 6:38. What contrasting behaviors are described in these passages? What are the results of these behaviors? What is God's instruction in this area?

5. Think about the environment in which you spend most of your waking hours. How would an increase in kindness by everyone affect it?

6. As you expand your "kindness horizons," what acts of kindness would you like to challenge yourself to do? How will you carry out these plans?

Appendix: "Mommy, please don't go!"

1. What are your thoughts on the subject of mothers staying at home versus working outside the home?

2. What are the good, better, and best reasons listed in this chapter for a mother to stay at home with her children?

3. How can mothers utilize the full potential of being at home to rear their children? Consult Deuteronomy 6:7–9, Proverbs 22:6, and 2 Timothy 3:15.

4. How strong is a mother's love? Tell from your own experience and read these passages: Exodus 2:1–10, I Samuel 1:9–28, 1 Kings 3:16–28, and Isaiah 49:15.

5. What are two rewards that a stay-at-home mom experiences? What are two difficulties?

6. a. If you are a stay-at-home mom, what is your greatest challenge? Draw up a step-by-step plan to meet this challenge.

b. If you work outside the home, what is your greatest challenge? Draw up a step-by-step plan to meet this challenge.

c. If your children are older, think about a stay-at-home mom or a working-outside-the-home mom who is frustrated and frazzled. How could you lend her a hand?

Scripture Index